Pesticides

Look for these and other books in the Lucent Overview series:

Pesticides

by Lisa Yount

OUR ENDANGERED PLANET

LUCENT *Overview Series*

TO STUART
no longer a pest

Library of Congress Cataloging-in-Publication Data

Yount, Lisa.
    Pesticides / Lisa Yount.
        p.   cm. — (Lucent overview series)
    Includes bibliographical references (p.   ) and index.
    ISBN 1-56006-156-1 (acid free)
    1. Pesticides—Juvenile literature.   2. Pesticides—Environmental
aspects—Juvenile literature. 3. Agricultural pests—Control—
Juvenile literature. [1. Pesticides.]   I. Title.   II. Series.
SB951.13.Y68   1995
363.73'84—dc20   94-26603
                                                                      CIP
                                                                       AC

Copyright © 1995 by Lucent Books, Inc.
P.O. Box 289011, San Diego, CA 92198-9011
Printed in the U.S.A.

Contents

FEDERAL/STATE GOVERNMENT

INSECT TRAP

PLEASE DO NOT DISTURB

Introduction

EVEN IN THE MOST PEACEFUL of times, human beings are fighting a war. That war has gone on as long as people have existed. In this battle the fight is for comfort, food, homes, and sometimes lives. The enemies are the plants and animals that humans call pests. A pest, from the human point of view, is any plant or animal that makes people ill or destroys food and possessions.

The war against pests is part of the competition built into nature. All living things except green plants must get food from other living things. Each living thing tries to protect itself from being eaten or otherwise harmed. People and the pests they attack are just both trying to survive.

The costs of humanity's ongoing fight against pests

Like all wars, the war against pests can have terrible costs, whether humanity loses or wins. If humanity loses the fight against mosquitoes, for instance, people will die of malaria or other diseases these insects carry. If humanity loses the fight against pests that destroy food, people will starve.

But winning—or seeming to win—the pest war also carries a price. In the 1940s scientists created

(Opposite page) An employee of the Florida Department of Agriculture holds a fruit fly trap before hanging it on a grapefruit tree. Fruit flies cause much devastation to citrus trees.

The leaves of a strawberry plant undergo thorough inspection for infestation. Pesticides prevent infestation but can also cause health problems.

new pesticides, or pest-killing chemicals, that promised an end to food loss and insect-carried disease. People soon learned, however, that these chemicals can poison not only pests but also songbirds and insects that destroy unwanted insects. They can even kill the crop plants they are supposed to protect. Pesticides can poison workers who apply them. They may harm people who eat food treated with them. Strange as it seems, they can also make pest problems worse.

By killing disease-carrying insects and destroying pests that ruin food, modern pesticides have saved untold lives. But they have also raised questions about risks to human health and the environment.

Finding the answers to these questions is not easy, but it is important. Choices we make about pesticides reflect our feelings about technology and nature. Those choices will have major effects on human health and the health of the earth.

1

The Everlasting War

And the Lord brought an east wind upon the land . . . and . . . the east wind brought the locusts. . . .

For they covered the face of the whole earth, so that the land was darkened; and they did eat every herb of the land, and all the fruit of the trees . . . ; and there remained not any green thing in the trees, or in the herbs of the field, through all the land of Egypt.

Exodus 10:13, 15

FARMERS TODAY SEEING their crops devoured by clouds of locusts, a kind of grasshopper, might well feel that the insects were a punishment sent by God, just as the Bible described. Locust swarms still sweep through North Africa, the Middle East, and India. They can eat more in a day than a village of five hundred people consumes in a year.

(Opposite page) A locust swarm fifteen miles wide and fifty miles long darkens the sky over Karachi, Pakistan. A swarm of this size can strip every tree and devour every blade of grass in its path.

The threat of pests

Locusts are just one of the pests that have destroyed food and threatened lives throughout human history. Many pests, like locusts, are insects. Beetles, weevils, and caterpillars attack grain, fruit trees, and other food plants. Flies,

11

Rodents destroy supplies of grain after making holes in the sacks. Destruction to the foods people eat is caused by more than just insects.

fleas, lice, and mosquitoes carry germs that cause disease.

Other plants and animals can be pests as well. Plantlike microorganisms called fungi turn ears of wheat or rye into clumps of black, foul-smelling dust. Weeds compete with crop plants for sunlight, water, soil nutrients, and space. Mice and rats eat stored grain and other food supplies. Coyotes and other wild animals attack cattle or sheep.

Only a tiny fraction of living things do humans any harm. Less than 0.1 percent of insect species are pests, for example. Still, pests have caused major disasters. Between 1345 and 1351 bubonic plague, or the Black Death, killed more than a fourth of the people in Europe. Fleas that live on rats carry the bacteria that cause this disease. In the 1840s a fungus destroyed potato crops in Belgium, France, England, and Ireland. Its effects were worst in Ireland, where potatoes were most people's only food. More than a million people—

about 12 percent of Ireland's population—died of hunger or disease between 1845 and 1860. Another million and a half left their homes for other countries.

The first pest controllers

Dealing with pests has always been part of human life. The earliest humans no doubt slapped at mosquitoes and biting flies. Chimpanzees comb each other's hair to pick out lice. Early people most likely did the same.

People probably did not think much about pest control, though, until they became farmers. About ten thousand years ago, people in the Middle East, Asia, and Central America began to sow the seeds of edible plants. The plants were harvested, and new ones grew up in the same place the next

An engraving depicts the backbreaking work of digging for potatoes in Ireland. The blight that destroyed Ireland's potato crop led to massive starvation.

A seventeenth-century rat catcher holds aloft a flag advertising his services. Throughout history, people have tried to get rid of pests.

year. With a dependable food supply, the human population expanded. So did the populations of insects and other living things that ate the same plants. People realized that they faced competition for their food. They began to fight back.

The five main kinds of pest control are physical, cultural, genetic, biological, and chemical. All started in ancient times. All are still used today.

Some of the simplest pest control methods, as well as some sophisticated ones, are physical or mechanical. The ancient Greeks (500 B.C.) hung nets around their beds to keep mosquitoes out. They painted sticky rings around the bases of fruit trees to stop insects from crawling up to the fruit. Celtic people in Spain stored grain in houselike buildings that stood on posts topped by circular stones, which kept the grain safe from rats.

Cultural pest control methods take advantage of the way farm crops are cultivated or grown. Experience long ago taught farmers to grow some crops early in the season, before pests matured. They grew other crops late, after pests had starved. In some places they flooded or burned fields at certain times to destroy weeds. Later farmers broke up soil with plows to kill insects and other pests that lived in the ground. Planting several crops in the same field made pests hunt longer for food plants. The different plants also gave homes to the pests' natural enemies. Starting in the Middle Ages (around A.D. 800), farmers in Europe began to use the same land to plant different crops in different years. This practice, called crop rotation, starved out some pests.

More ways to control pests

Farmers also noticed that in plants and animals, just as in people, offspring frequently resembled the parents. They therefore saved the seeds of only the healthiest plants to sow for the next year's crop. They let only the healthiest cattle and other domestic animals breed. In this way they produced plants and animals with inherited, or genetic, power to resist pests.

Some ancient peoples used other living things to control pests. Examples of this practice, which is called biological control, include sending pigs or goats into fields to eat weeds and keeping cats to catch rats and mice. In China around A.D. 300, growers of citrus trees placed the nests of certain ants in the trees. The growers even built bamboo bridges to help the ants move from tree to tree. The ants ate insects that otherwise would have damaged the valuable fruit crop.

Using chemicals to kill pests is also a very ancient form of control. The Sumerians, who lived in what is now Iraq, used sulfur to poison insects before 2500 B.C. The Chinese began making insecticides (insect-killing chemicals) from plants about 1200 B.C. They also used compounds of mercury and arsenic, two poisonous metals, to kill lice.

New pest problems

Pest control methods changed little for hundreds of years. When new pest problems appeared in the nineteenth century, however, new methods of fighting pests began to develop.

European farms were growing larger in the 1800s. Farmers often filled field after field with the same kind of crop. This farming practice is called monoculture. Such crops were most often grown for sale rather than to feed the farmer's family. Monoculture gave pests that attacked popular crops an unlimited food supply, making some pest problems worse.

Pest problems also grew as railroads and steamships made travel easier. Accidentally or on purpose, people brought other living things with them when they moved to different countries. Many of these plants and animals had been harmless in their old homes. In a new environment, however, they sometimes found a large food supply and no natural enemies. Their populations exploded, creating new pests.

A Frenchman named Leopold Trouvelot, who wanted to start a silk-making industry in Massachusetts, brought a terrible pest to the United States in 1869. Silk is made from the cocoons of a certain kind, or species, of moths. The cocoons are produced by caterpillars called silkworms. Instead of importing silkworms, Trouvelot selected a European species of moth that also made silky cocoons. When a storm overturned their cage, the moths flew away. They spread so widely that they soon became known as "gypsy moths." Their caterpillars stripped leaves from oaks and similar trees. One observer wrote that in a heavily infested town, "in the still, summer nights the sound of their feeding could plainly be heard."

Introducing a new food crop to a native insect could be just as bad. Before the 1850s, Colorado

A Frenchman who wished to start his own silk-making industry in Massachusetts used a variety of European moth rather than the traditional silkworm (pictured). The moths escaped during a storm, rapidly multiplied, and destroyed tree leaves.

potato beetles lived on "buffalo fur," a wild plant of the potato family. When settlers brought potatoes to Colorado, the beetles found the new plants much tastier. Before long they were attacking potato plants throughout the country.

To fight these new problems, scientists and farmers invented new methods of pest control. Some were old techniques used in new ways. Instead of picking bugs from plants by hand, for example, farmers in 1867 could use a horse-drawn vehicle that knocked beetles out of potato plants, then smashed them between heavy rollers.

Ladybugs to the rescue

Biological control also had one great success during the decades after the Civil War. A slow-moving, fluffy-looking insect called the cottony-cushion scale first appeared on California citrus trees in the late 1860s. Twenty years later it was a major pest. A scientist named Charles V. Riley wondered what enemies might have controlled the scale in Australia, its native country. In 1888 he sent an assistant, Albert Koebele, to Australia to find out.

Koebele found two natural enemies. One was a tiny fly that laid eggs in the scale insect's body. When the eggs hatched, the fly's wormlike young or larvae used the scale for food. The fly was a parasite, a living thing that lives in and eats living plants or animals. The other enemy was the vedalia beetle, a kind of ladybug. The beetle was a predator. It killed the scale insects and then ate them, just as a fox eats a rabbit.

Koebele brought a few of the flies and beetles back to California. The flies did not thrive in their new home, but the beetles did. In a year and a half, the descendants of Koebele's 140

A vedalia beetle eats destructive citrus scale insects. These remarkable bugs are used in a form of biological warfare— using one species to devastate another.

vedalia beetles had cleaned most of the scale insects from the state's citrus trees.

"Spray, O spray"

Most farmers, however, knew little about biological control. Instead, they turned to a new group of chemical pest killers. The most popular were made from poisonous metals. Paris green, a compound of arsenic and copper, was the first to be applied. Farmers in Europe and the United States began using this substance around 1867. It worked by killing insects that chewed leaves on which it had been sprayed. In the early twentieth century another arsenic compound, lead arsenate, largely replaced Paris green.

Another metal-based poison was first used in France. A fungus called powdery mildew threatened the grapes of France's world-famous wine industry in the mid-nineteenth century. Around 1885 a French farmer trying to keep passers-by from stealing his grapes found a cure for the mildew. To discourage unauthorized sampling, the farmer coated grapes by the roadside with a repulsive-looking blue mixture of copper sulfate and lime (calcium carbonate). He found that his painted grapes stayed free of fungus as well as thieves. His compound came to be called Bordeaux mixture, after the part of France in which it was discovered. It is still a widely used fungicide (fungus-killing chemical).

Compared to other forms of pest control, the new chemicals were cheap, effective, and easy to use. Farmers dusted them onto plants as a powder or mixed them with liquid and sprayed them. Spraying machines began to be used about 1880.

Nineteenth-century workers harvest grapes in France. A French farmer accidentally discovered an effective cure for powdery mildew, which plagued the grapes. His solution also discouraged thieves from stealing the crop.

Workers use convenient insecticide sprayers in 1938. The ease of using pesticides quickly led to their overuse.

Most were just backpack tanks with rubber hoses and nozzles. The machines were awkward, but they and the pesticides they carried soon became farmers' favorite weapons against pests. A poem printed in a 1906 issue of *Entomological News* expressed the farmers' enthusiasm:

> Spray for blight, and spray for rot,
> Take good care of what you've got;
> Spray, farmers, spray with care,
> Spray, O spray the buglets there.

Some people worried about the safety of these poisonous compounds. When overused, arsenic pesticides sometimes killed bees, livestock, and even the crops they were supposed to protect. No one doubted that they could poison people, too. Still, experts could not agree about whether the tiny amount of pesticide residue, or leftover material, on sprayed fruits and vegetables was harmful. It seldom was enough to cause acute, or sudden, poisoning. But could small amounts build up in the body and cause chronic, or long-term, illness? Some scientists said yes. Others said no. Meanwhile, farmers insisted that any health risks from arsenic in food were nothing compared to the benefits of the pesticides in saving crops.

People in the early part of the twentieth century did not worry as much about what they ate and drank as we do today. The first U.S. law governing the contents of foods and medicines was passed in 1906. Called the Pure Food and Drug Act, this law simply required that processed foods, drinks, and drugs be labeled correctly. It was illegal for them to contain any substances not listed on the label. In 1910 a similar law concerning pesticides was passed. Neither law limited the amount of pesticide that could remain on food. Only in 1926 did the government set a limit on the amount of arsenic residue permitted on food.

People argued more about pesticide safety in the 1930s. World War II, however, overrode all concerns about trace poisons in the food supply. By the time the war ended in 1945, no one cared whether arsenic pesticides were harmful because the compounds were no longer much used. They had been replaced by pesticides of new kinds that were far more effective—and possibly far more dangerous.

2

Bountiful Harvest or Silent Spring?

IN THE SUMMER OF 1943, a case of a deadly disease called typhus appeared in the Italian city of Naples. Body pests called lice carry the microorganism that causes this disease, which is common in crowded, dirty conditions such as those of wartime. By the end of December, 371 people in Naples had typhus. World War II was at its height in Europe, and military leaders feared that a typhus epidemic would sweep through the city, possibly killing thousands.

Stopping an epidemic

About a year earlier, the U.S. Department of Agriculture (USDA) had received a sample of a new pesticide from Geigy, a Swiss firm. The chemical had a jaw-breaking name: dichloro-diphenyltrichloroethane, which was quickly shortened to DDT. Paul Müller, a Geigy chemist, had discovered DDT in 1939. The substance killed most insects he tried it on. Hoping for a way to stop the spread of insect-carried diseases among the troops, the USDA began its own research based on Müller's results. The U.S. agency found that a powder containing 10 percent DDT, dusted onto the body, killed lice for weeks.

(Opposite page) A soldier dusts his clothing with DDT during World War II. Initially used to kill disease-carrying lice, DDT was later found to be harmful to a wide range of animals.

23

In 1944, a U.S. Department of Agriculture chemist analyzes different mixes of DDT to determine its insect-killing power.

Military health workers set up DDT dusting stations all over Naples. They powdered people, clothes, bedding, or anywhere else lice might hide. They dusted again every few weeks. By early February 1944, the typhus epidemic was stopped.

After that, all Allied personnel (soldiers of the countries, including the United States, that opposed Germany, Italy, and Japan in the war) carried cans of DDT powder. In the tropics, buildings were sprayed with liquid DDT to kill mosquitoes. Mosquitoes can carry malaria, a serious blood disease. Thanks to DDT, few soldiers got this disease during the war. Brig. Gen. James Simmons said that DDT was "the War's greatest contribution to the future health of the world." Paul Müller won a Nobel Prize in 1948 for his discovery.

Killer of killers

When the war was over, American home-owners demanded the miracle chemical. "The army's new insect-killer has nearly every house-holder pawing the ground in eagerness," a magazine reported in 1945. DDT was called the "killer of killers" and "the atomic bomb of the insect world."

Farmers and foresters were even more excited. DDT slew archenemies such as the gypsy moth and the cotton boll weevil. And anything DDT did not get, a host of other new pesticides would. Most were chemicals made from petroleum (oil). Some, called organochlorines, were related to

Homeowners began using DDT, termed the "killer of killers," after World War II. With her infant inches away, a woman sprays a DDT "bomb" in her home to prevent insects.

DDT. These substances included chlordane, dieldrin, and aldrin. Others, called organophosphates, had been discovered by the Germans during war research on nerve gas. They included parathion and malathion. Both groups of pesticides poison insects' nervous systems. A new herbicide (plant killer) called 2,4-D destroyed weeds.

Like the old arsenic compounds, the new pesticides were cheap and easy to use. As far as anyone knew, the new compounds were far less poisonous than the old. And above all, they were effective. In tests, 87 of 100 unsprayed apples contained codling moth larvae, for instance. Only 4 of 100 apples sprayed with Guthion (an organophosphate) had such "worms." The new pesticides worked equally well in farms, forests, gardens, homes, and large buildings.

Making pesticides became a profitable business. Americans used five times as much pesticide in 1960 as they had in 1945. Most people stopped using other forms of pest control.

Pesticides on the farm

American farms during the 1940s and 1950s were more productive than ever before. The new pesticides were one reason for this success. New fertilizers, better farm machines, and new breeds of crop plants also helped to create the farm boom.

Large farms produced the most. Their owners, wealthy people or companies, could afford the newest chemicals and best machines. Most owners of small family farms could not. Partly because of this, many small farms failed.

Surviving farmers found that they needed more and more pesticides. One reason was that most large farms grew a single, high-profit crop. Such monoculture led to an increase in pests and thus

in the need for pesticides. Another reason was that the farms produced more than people wanted to buy. Prices for farm goods therefore fell. The government then paid farmers to stop growing crops on part of their land. To maximize their profit, the farmers grew as much as they could on the rest. That meant using more pesticides. One critic called this situation "a pesticide salesman's dream."

Farmers and pesticide makers thus came to depend on each other. If farmers had pest problems, they asked pesticide salespeople for advice. The salespeople, of course, said to use more pesticide. They told the farmers to spray on a schedule (say, once every two weeks), whether the farmers saw pests or not.

The USDA, whose duties included regulation of pesticides, did little to regulate their production

Growing methods of the 1940s and 1950s required the use of more pesticides than ever before.

A farmer displays the chemicals—fertilizers and pesticides—he uses in an average year on his seventy-eight acres. At the time this photo was taken, during the 1950s, farmers were increasing their dependence on chemicals to increase crop yields.

or use. The main law governing pesticides, the Federal Insecticide, Fungicide, and Rodenticide Act (FIFRA), was passed in 1947. Like earlier laws relating to food and drug products, it merely required that pesticides be labeled correctly. It said nothing about testing them for safety or controlling their use.

Total victory?

The USDA itself soon became the country's biggest pesticide user. In the late 1950s it launched huge spraying campaigns against two insect pests, the gypsy moth and the fire ant. In those days people expected "total victory on the insect front," as *Popular Science* put it. The campaigns therefore were designed to eradicate, or wipe out, these pests. Gypsy moths caused great damage, but fire ants, which live in the South, were mostly a nuisance. Their bites are painful, and their large nest mounds can break farm machines. Many southerners were surprised, though, to learn that the USDA thought the ants a major pest.

The gypsy moth campaign was to cover three million acres of land in four northeastern states. In April 1957 planes began spraying a mist of DDT mixed with oil over the forests where the moths lived. The planes also sprayed farms, marshes, and suburbs. The fire ant campaign sprayed an even larger area with dieldrin, chlordane, and heptachlor. These organochlorines were at least forty times as poisonous as DDT. In both campaigns, people's land was sprayed whether they liked it or not.

A man sprays for gypsy moths in Palo Alto, California. During the 1950s, the federal government formed a plan to completely eradicate the moths.

The terrible devastation reflected in this photo reveals why people were so eager to eradicate the gypsy moth.

Some people protested against these large campaigns. It was a smaller pest "battle," however, that set into motion events that forever changed the way people felt about pesticides. In the summer of 1957, while parts of the Northeast were being drenched in DDT to control gypsy moths, planes sprayed the same mixture of chemicals over Plymouth County, Massachusetts. Their aim was to kill mosquitoes in marshes. Among the places they sprayed was a bird sanctuary owned by Olga Huckins and her husband. Soon after the spraying, the Huckinses found their land littered with dead songbirds.

The birth of *Silent Spring*

Olga Huckins described the tragedy in a letter to the Boston *Herald*. She sent a copy of her letter to an old friend named Rachel Carson, who had worked for the U.S. Fish and Wildlife Service for sixteen years. Carson, a biologist with a master's degree from Johns Hopkins University, was also a respected essayist and a best-selling author. Her book *The Sea Around Us* vividly described the ocean and its complex life. Huckins asked Carson if she knew anyone who could stop the spraying.

Carson was deeply disturbed by what Huckins had told her. The news from Massachusetts provided dramatic confirmation of other reports she had heard, indicating that pesticides killed wildlife. She decided to write about the dangers of pesticide misuse. Later Carson said:

> There would be no peace for me if I kept silent. Everything which meant most to me as a naturalist was being threatened. . . . I wanted to do more than merely express concern: I wanted to demonstrate that that concern was well founded.

Carson spent the next four and a half years gathering scientific evidence that would, she believed, put her claims on an "unshakable foundation."

Long-lasting poisons

Carson's work was published first as three articles in the *New Yorker* magazine, beginning on June 16, 1962. It then appeared as a book, *Silent Spring*, in September.

Carson explained the book's title in its first chapter, "A Fable for Tomorrow." In this imagined scene, an unnamed pesticide makes plants and animals in a small town sicken or die. Spring is silent because no birds sing. Streams are empty of fish. Roadside plants are "browned and withered." Farmers' cattle, pets, and families become ill. "I know of no community that has experienced all the misfortunes I describe," Carson admitted. Her fable was not a report but a worst-case picture. She used it to shock readers into paying attention to the real disasters the rest of her book described.

Biologist and writer Rachel Carson dedicated herself to researching the effects of pesticides on the environment.

Carson had doubts about the safety of all pesticides. She was most concerned, however, about DDT and the other organochlorines. (She called them chlorinated hydrocarbons.) Since these chemicals stay active long after they have been applied, they can be spread far from where they are sprayed, carrying their poisoning power with them. They can be absorbed into soil, blown by wind, leached into groundwater, or washed into rivers.

The organochlorines also remain active after being taken in by living things. They are stored in fat. Carson therefore thought small doses of the chemicals could in time add up to amounts large enough to cause illness. The compounds also can move from one living thing to another along the food chain, from plants to plant-eating animals to meat-eating animals. Each living thing's body concentrates the poison. This means that each link in the chain gets a larger dose than the one below. An animal at the top of the chain may take in enough poison to cause sickness or even death.

Harmful to wildlife

Pesticides harmed wildlife even when they did not kill, Carson claimed. Soon after pesticide spraying became widespread, people saw a large drop in the number of young birds in some sprayed areas. They found that many adult birds were not building nests or laying eggs. Few of the eggs that were laid would hatch. The eggs had shells so thin that the adult birds broke them just by sitting on them. Carson could not prove that these problems were caused by pesticides, but she believed they were.

Carson pointed out that people also had been killed or made seriously ill by exposure to large amounts of pesticides. She suspected that even small amounts could lead to chronic illness. The

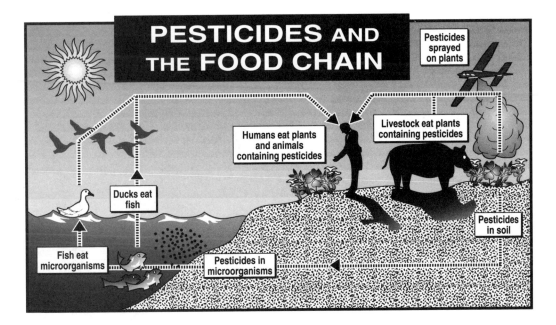

PESTICIDES AND THE FOOD CHAIN

Pesticides sprayed on plants

Humans eat plants and animals containing pesticides

Livestock eat plants containing pesticides

Ducks eat fish

Pesticides in soil

Fish eat microorganisms

Pesticides in microorganisms

human body, like those of animals, stores and concentrates organochlorines. Tests on animals showed that these chemicals could harm the nervous system and liver. They might cause cancer and birth defects. Carson could not prove that this also happened in people, but humans are much like other mammals. Something that harmed a rat probably could harm a person, too.

Need for a better way

Finally, Carson said, pesticides were no longer as good at killing pests as people thought. Often a few pest insects in a field happened to have an inherited power to resist a pesticide. Their bodies might break down the poison into harmless substances, for example. After repeated pesticide sprayings, only resistant insects would be left. At the time Carson wrote her book, 137 insect species had become resistant to one or more pesticides.

Carson urged use of biological control, which was based on natural relationships such as that

Gordon Brooks/*Yankee Magazine*, May 1963.

"Just say the blow was inflicted by a blunt instrument"

between predator and prey. Biological control methods usually harmed only pests. In addition, pests could not develop resistance to them. Thus, Carson said, these methods were not only safer but, in the long run, cheaper and more effective than chemical controls.

Carson stressed that she did not demand a ban on all pesticides. She just wanted more care in their use and more testing for possible harmful effects. Only the organochlorines, because of their persistence, should perhaps be banned.

Respecting the web of life

Carson believed that pesticide overuse raised questions that were "not only scientific but moral." First, she said, overuse showed a lack of understanding of the "web of life" that makes up the natural world. "In nature nothing exists alone,"

Carson wrote. The actions of each part of the web—which includes human beings—affect all the others. The effects are often unexpected. Thus pesticide users intend to kill only pest insects, but they may also kill birds because birds eat the insects.

Worse still, thoughtless pesticide use suggested that people did not care what they did to nature. Pesticides were just a few of the dangerous chemicals with which humans were polluting the world. Such pollution, Carson felt, reflected a feeling that humans were more important than any other living things. At the end of *Silent Spring* she wrote:

> The "control of nature" is a phrase conceived in arrogance [excessive pride], born of the . . . age of biology and philosophy when it was supposed that nature exists for the convenience of man. . . . It is our alarming misfortune that so primitive a science has armed itself with the most modern and terrible weapons. . . . In turning them against the insects it has also turned them against the earth.

Angry reactions

Reaction to Carson's book was immediate and fierce. One pesticide firm threatened a lawsuit, although it backed down after a scientist hired by Carson's publisher said that her information was accurate. Another published an article, "The Desolate Year," modeled after the opening "fable" in *Silent Spring*. The article claimed that famines and epidemics would occur if all pesticides were banned, ignoring the fact that Carson had not called for a such ban. Food processors, farm bureaus, and USDA officials also complained. Some called Carson's book "science fiction" because of its fictional opening.

Most of Carson's critics did not argue with her facts. They accused her, however, of using "emotion-fanning" phrases such as "chain of evil." They also complained that she described the

Carson's research led her to write the book Silent Spring, *which detailed the effects of pesticides on populations of birds, fish, and other animals. It also speculated on pesticides' effects on human health. Carson found that the pesticide weakened birds' eggshells, making them brittle and easily broken.*

harm but not the good done by pesticides. Carson did not deny these charges. She had never claimed to be balanced or "objective."

Carson's critics also claimed, with some truth, that her conclusions sometimes went beyond her evidence. Some wildlife damage she blamed on pesticides could have been caused by other things. Other pollutants might have killed fish in rivers, for instance. Loss of places to live might have cut the numbers of some birds. When discussing pesticides' dangers to health, Carson clearly was describing mostly possibilities, not proven facts. Carson and her opponents agreed that no one knew much about how small amounts of pesticides affected people or animals.

Most of Carson's main points, however, were hard to deny. The majority of reviewers, including scientists, supported her. So did most of her many readers. (*Silent Spring* sold more than a million copies and was translated into twelve languages.) Carson was not the first person to say that pesticides might be dangerous. She was the first, though, to describe the possible dangers in terms the public understood. Her wide-ranging supporting evidence and skillful, passionate writing made people listen to her message.

Carson's most impressive support came from the President's Science Advisory Committee. This group, which included many famous scientists, had been asked by President John F. Kennedy to look into pesticides after Carson's *New Yorker* articles appeared. The committee's report, presented in mid-1963, reached most of the same conclusions as *Silent Spring*. When the report came out, CBS newsman Eric Sevareid said:

> Miss Carson had two immediate aims. One was to alert the public; the second, to build a fire under the Government. She accomplished the first months ago. Tonight's report by the Presidential panel is . . . evidence that she has also accomplished the second.

Sevareid was too optimistic. Carson herself pointed out that "this excellent report . . . must now be translated into action." Carson did not live to see much of that action, however. She died of cancer on April 14, 1964, at the age of fifty-six. Even so, changes slowly took place.

The fruits of *Silent Spring* and the beginning of increased environmental awareness

Some of the changes were in the public. Nature protection groups such as the Audubon Society had existed long before Carson wrote *Silent Spring*, but their membership had been small.

"After we read Silent Spring, *we decided to live and let live."*

Berry's World reprinted by permission of NEA, Inc.

Most people seldom thought about nature or the environment. Carson's writing woke them, not only to the dangers of pesticides, but to the importance of acting responsibly toward the natural world. Some people joined the older groups and made them more active in politics. Others formed new groups, such as the Environmental Defense Fund. In 1972 a writer noted, "Alarm about the environment sprang from nowhere to major proportions in a few short years." The start of that alarm can be traced largely to *Silent Spring.*

Other changes occurred in government. Carson had called for "an independent board . . . to be set up at the level of the Executive Offices" to deal with environmental matters. In 1970 President Richard Nixon set up such an agency. It was the Environmental Protection Agency (EPA). One writer called the EPA "the extended shadow of *Silent Spring.*"

In 1972, in a revision of FIFRA, Congress declared that in the future the EPA rather than the USDA would regulate pesticides. Congress ordered the EPA to carry out extensive safety tests before approving a pesticide for use.

The EPA was not long in acting. In the same year it received authority to regulate pesticides, the agency banned the use of DDT in the United States. The ban did not prevent American companies from making the chemical and selling it to other countries, however. Most other organochlorines were banned in the United States later in the decade. These bans, too, seem to have been mostly a result of *Silent Spring*. One government expert has said, "There is no question that *Silent Spring* prompted the federal government to take action against . . . persistent pesticides several years before it otherwise would have moved."

3

Pesticides Today

T HE OUTCRY FOLLOWING *Silent Spring* did not stop or even greatly slow pesticide use in the United States or elsewhere in the world. Indeed, pesticide use in this country doubled between 1964 and 1977. Since then it has leveled off. For the most part, world use has followed a similar pattern.

Kinds of pesticides

Pesticides used today can be grouped in several ways—for example, by the kinds of pests they kill. The most common pesticides are herbicides, insecticides, and fungicides. Other kinds include rodenticides, which kill rats and mice. Molluscicides kill snails and slugs. Nematocides kill soil-dwelling worms, called nematodes, which harm some plants.

Americans use far more herbicides than any other kind of pesticide. Two herbicides, atrazine and alachlor, are the most widely used pesticides in the United States. One reason for the widespread use of herbicides on farms is "no-till" farming. Instead of killing weeds by tilling land, or breaking up soil with a plow, many farmers just spray fields with herbicide before crop plants

(Opposite page) In stark contrast to the days when soldiers dusted their uniforms and homeowners sprayed their rooms with DDT, a farmer wears a protective mask and clothing while he sprays a field of snow peas in California.

come up. No-till farming saves work and cuts down soil erosion, but it requires heavy chemical use.

Some herbicides, such as 2,4-D, make plants grow abnormally and die. Others, such as atrazine, stop plants from making food or chemicals they need. Paraquat dries out plant leaves when triggered by sunlight. Some herbicides kill only plants of certain kinds. Others kill all plants.

Insecticides are the next largest group of pesticides. Most are nerve poisons. Most members of one older group, the organochlorines, are no longer used in the United States. Some organophosphates, such as malathion, are still used. A third older group of insecticides is the carbamates. This category includes aldicarb and carbofuran.

Most of the pyrethroids, the newest large group of insecticides, came into use in the 1970s. They are artificial forms of a poison made by a type of chrysanthemum. (The natural form, pyrethrum, is also used.) Pyrethroids, which are contained in many household and livestock sprays, knock pest insects down quickly but are not as toxic as most other insecticides.

Fungicides are the third main kind of pesticide. Some protect seeds before planting. Others are sprayed on fruits and vegetables to keep them from spoiling. Fungicides include copper compounds such as Bordeaux mixture and newer chemicals such as maneb.

Pesticide mixtures

The part of a commercial pesticide that kills pests is the active ingredient. A commercial pesticide may have one or more of these substances, but they are just a small part of the pesticide that is sold. The rest consists of inert or inactive ingredients, which help the active ingredients dissolve, spread, or stick to plants or insects. Inert ingredients may be water, oil, clay, or more complex chemicals.

The blend of active and inert ingredients in a commercial pesticide is called the formulation. Many formulations include the same active ingredients in different amounts and with different inert ingredients. By 1990 the EPA had registered or approved only about six hundred active pesticide ingredients. These were used, however, in some twenty thousand different formulations or products. The word *formulation* also is used to refer to the process of preparing a pesticide mixture for sale or use.

Applying pesticides

Pesticides may be applied in different ways. Spraying and dusting are the most common. About three-fourths of insecticides are sprayed. In homes and greenhouses, pesticides are often

Workers spray insecticides on strawberry plants. Spraying and dusting are the two most common methods of applying pesticides.

sprayed from aerosol cans. Some farmers still use old-fashioned backpack sprayers in their fields, but more modern devices are available. Some newer sprayers put out droplets of pesticide charged with static electricity. The charge pulls the drops toward plants. Such sprayers cut down the amount of pesticide used.

Machines or planes often spray or dust large farms. Machines can treat several rows of crops at once. Planes can cover an even larger area quickly, but much of their spray is wasted. One study showed that less than 0.1 percent of insecticide sprayed by air reached pest insects.

Some pesticides are applied in other ways. Small pellets, or granules, may be scattered onto the soil from a handheld tube. Pesticides that control underground pests are injected into the soil. Some pesticides are mixed with bait that attracts pest insects or animals.

Pesticide use worldwide

In 1991, the EPA estimated that about 1.1 billion pounds of active pesticide ingredients were used in the United States. That is a little over four pounds for each person in the country. If wood preservatives, disinfectants, and sulfur products were included, the amount would be twice as great. Users spent about $8.3 billion on these chemicals.

The EPA says 76 percent of U.S. pesticides were used in farming. However, only about 24 percent of U.S. farmland was treated with herbicides, 9 percent with insecticides, and 1 percent with fungicides. Cotton, corn, soybeans, and fruits and vegetables are the crops most often treated with pesticides.

Eighteen percent of U.S. pesticides were used in public, commercial, or industrial buildings: hotels, restaurants, factories, offices, schools, and

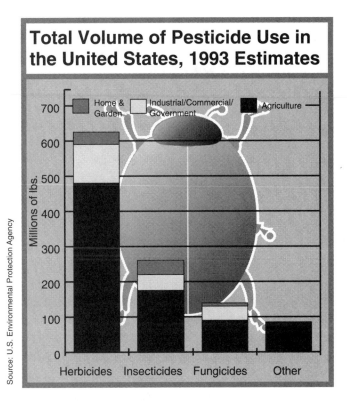

Total Volume of Pesticide Use in the United States, 1993 Estimates

Home & Garden

Industrial/Commercial/ Government

Agriculture

Millions of lbs.

700
600
500
400
300
200
100
0

Herbicides   Insecticides   Fungicides   Other

so on. The professional pest control operators who apply most such pesticides must be trained and licensed.

The remaining 6 percent of pesticides used in the United States were used in homes, lawns, and gardens. Most home pesticides are used against cockroaches, fleas, ants, or termites. Professional pest control operators apply some home pesticides, especially those used against termites. Homeowners use the rest. About sixty-nine million American households used pesticides in 1991. An EPA survey found that 85 percent of two thousand households had at least one pesticide. Most had one to five pesticides.

The EPA estimated that about 4.5 billion pounds of active pesticide ingredients were used worldwide in 1991. Their cost exceeded $25 billion. Four-fifths of the world's pesticides are used

A Costa Rican field worker sprays pesticides to control an infestation of crop-damaging insects. Developing countries account for almost a fifth of the world's pesticide use.

in developed or industrialized countries. The United States uses a little more than a third of the developed world's total. Europe uses most of the rest.

The United States exported about 0.4 billion pounds of active pesticide ingredients in 1991. That was almost a third of the amount it made. Most of the other pesticides in the world are made in western Europe. Bayer, a German chemical company, is the world's largest pesticide exporter.

The developing countries of the Third World use about a fifth of the world's pesticides. Third World countries use some pesticides to control insect-carried diseases. In 1955, for example, the World Health Organization (WHO) of the United Nations began an eight-year program to wipe out malaria worldwide. One writer called this program the "most ambitious and largest undertaking in public health history." At the program's peak, in the early 1960s, it covered 76 countries and sprayed 69,500 tons of pesticides in 100 million dwellings. The estimated number of malaria cases worldwide dropped from 300 million in 1946 to 120 million in the late 1960s, even though population in the treated areas doubled. By 1970 the

WHO program had prevented 2 billion malaria cases and saved 15 million lives. Less ambitious disease control programs continue today.

The Green Revolution

As in the developed world, most Third World pesticides are used in farming. In the 1950s, when these chemicals were introduced, they seemed to work miracles. Yields of many crops doubled or tripled.

Pesticides became still more important in the 1960s and 1970s, when a group of new farming technologies came to the Third World. These technologies and related advances promised to increase farmers' yields so much that they were called, collectively, the Green Revolution. People hoped this "revolution" would end poverty and hunger.

New types, or strains, of rice, wheat, and corn (maize) were at the core of the Green Revolution. These strains, developed in scientists' laboratories, produced more food per acre than anything

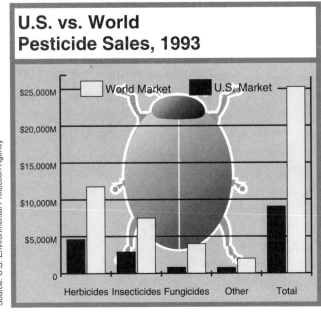

U.S. vs. World Pesticide Sales, 1993

World Market · U.S. Market

$25,000M
$20,000M
$15,000M
$10,000M
$5,000M
0

Herbicides · Insecticides · Fungicides · Other · Total

Source: U.S. Environmental Protection Agency

seen before. But they were less hardy than the old types. They needed large amounts of water, artificial fertilizer, and pesticides.

The Green Revolution turned out to be more helpful to rich farmers than to poor ones. Poor farmers often could not afford fertilizers and pesticides. In addition, their land did not have enough water for the new strains. Because such crops grew best in monoculture on large farms, wealthy agriculturalists bought or seized the land of poor farmers to expand their own businesses.

The same situation exists today, although more poor farmers and farmworkers now use pesticides. Most pesticides in the Third World are applied to crops grown for export, not to food crops for local people. Most money from the sale of the crops goes to rich landowners. A scientist from OXFAM (a British foreign aid group) has said, "Rather than feeding the hungry, pesticides [are] poisoning the hungry to feed the well fed."

Like farmers in the developed countries, Third World farmers have had great trouble with pests that acquire resistance to pesticides. They also have special problems in using pesticides safely. Many, relying on pesticide ads that promise high yields, use far more of the substances than they need to. In addition, they get most of their pest control advice from pesticide salespeople. Many Third World farmers have become dependent on pesticides, and even when they learn the dangers of these chemicals, they fear they will face disaster without them.

Creating a new pesticide

A pesticide active ingredient goes through a long, expensive development process before it can be sold. The National Agricultural Chemicals Association says that in the United States the process takes eight to ten years and costs $35

Overcome by a new viral insecticide, a cotton bollworm hangs from the boll of a treated cotton plant. All new insecticides are thoroughly tested under various conditions before they can be used commercially.

million to $50 million. Only one in about twenty thousand tested chemicals survives this series of procedures. The story is much the same in Europe.

The first step in the development process is screening, or looking for chemicals that might have pest-killing activity. Sometimes chemists test compounds similar to known pesticides. Sometimes they study chemicals in the bodies of pests, since substances that interfere with these chemicals may kill or weaken pests.

During the development process, a pesticide goes through more than 120 different tests. At first, chemical company scientists study small samples in laboratories and greenhouses. Later the tests are expanded to use larger amounts, applied on fields outdoors. Testing proceeds in several phases. At the end of each phase, the company evaluates the test results. It then decides whether to go on to the next phase.

Some tests explore how well the pesticide works against pests of different kinds. Some look for the best formulation and the most effective way to apply the pesticide. Scientists learn how long the chemical stays active and what happens to it when it breaks down. They find out how it spreads through the environment.

Above all, the pesticide is tested to see what harm it might do to nonpest animals. Outdoor tests show what kinds of wildlife eat or absorb the chemical and what happens to them. Laboratory tests show how much chemical is needed to kill test animals. Scientists also look for more subtle damage that leads to birth defects, cancer, or other illness. The results of tests on animals are used to predict dangers to humans.

EPA registration

When all the tests on a proposed pesticide have been completed, the manufacturer presents its results to the EPA and asks the agency to register the new substance. To be sold legally in the United States, a pesticide must be registered, and to gain registration, a company must show that the pesticide produces no "unreasonable adverse [harmful] effects" on nonpest animals or people.

The EPA may register a pesticide for either general or restricted use. If a pesticide is approved for general use, anyone may apply it. More dangerous pesticides are restricted. That is, only licensed pest control operators may use them. The EPA may approve a pesticide only for certain purposes. If reports of unexpected harm to people or wildlife appear after a pesticide has been registered, the agency can review the registration. Following an unfavorable review,

the EPA may ban the chemical for some or all uses.

How good is EPA regulation?

Different groups have opposing complaints about today's EPA regulations. Pesticide companies say the agency's rules are often hard to interpret. They feel the EPA requires some tests that are not really necessary. Testing, they say, is so expensive that it discourages the companies from developing new pesticides. Meeting the EPA testing requirements uses about one-fourth of the money spent by American pesticide companies on research and development of new products. The companies also say

An entomologist examines gypsy moth eggs in cold storage as part of a research effort to develop a new pesticide. Many pesticide manufacturers complain that EPA testing requirements are too stringent, repetitious, and expensive.

that the EPA has banned formerly approved pesticides without good reason.

Some health and environmental groups, on the other hand, say that the EPA rules are strict only on paper. They would like the EPA to check the results of pesticide companies' test reports by doing tests of its own. They also think the EPA should add more tests to those now required. They say, for example, that so-called inert ingredients should be tested for possible harm to human health. A biologist who used to work for the EPA says bluntly, "People . . . think there's this big federal apparatus safeguarding the environment. . . . That's not the case at all. The whole pesticide-registration system is a sham." A 1992 report by the U.S. General Accounting Office echoed most of the environmentalists' complaints about EPA regulation.

The EPA faces one special problem: Most pesticides sold today were approved many years ago, when far fewer tests were required, and before today's sensitive testing methods had been invented. Some of these pesticides may not meet the EPA's present requirements. Because of this problem, in 1988 Congress ordered the EPA to reregister older pesticides, applying the new tests to them.

Pesticide companies, which must pay part of the costs of reregistration, have stopped selling many pesticides rather than spend money in this way. Even so, the work of reregistration has overwhelmed the EPA. The job was supposed to be completed by 1994. By 1993, however, only twenty-seven older pesticides had been reregistered. Hundreds more remain untested.

To improve its regulation of pesticides, the EPA will need more money than it has now. Congress could provide this by raising taxes, shifting money from other programs, or charging fees to pesticide makers or users. Americans will have to decide whether they want to pay for more testing by the federal government or use the money for something else, such as developing alternatives to pesticides.

CAUTION
RESTRICTED
PESTICIDE

4

Are Pesticides Dangerous?

MORE THAN THIRTY YEARS after *Silent Spring*, people are still asking the questions Rachel Carson raised. Are pesticides dangerous to the environment? Are they dangerous to human health?

Dangers to the environment

Pesticides have not confirmed Carson's worst fears. Still, later research has supported many of her claims about the dangers of pesticides to the environment.

There is good evidence that DDT poisoning made some birds lay eggs with thin shells, for example. Experiments showed that DDT can interfere with birds' use of calcium, the mineral that makes bones and eggshells hard. After DDT was banned in the United States, bird species that had been laying thin-shelled eggs began to lay normal eggs. DDT is not the only cause of thin eggshells, however. One European bird species showed such thinning because of too little calcium in its diet.

Pesticides are tested and used more carefully today than in Carson's time, and large wildlife kills caused by pesticides are not common in

(Opposite page) A sign warns people away from an area that has been treated with pesticides. The World Health Organization estimates that over a million people are poisoned by pesticides each year.

developed countries. Environmentalists say they do still occur, however. For example, granular carbofuran, a carbamate insecticide, was banned in Virginia in 1991 because it killed birds. One estimate said the chemical poisoned two million birds a year. Citizens' groups pushed for the ban after finding dead eagles and other birds around carbofuran-treated fields. Tests confirmed that the compound had caused the birds' death. *National Wildlife* magazine said that Virginia's ban of carbofuran was "the first time anywhere [that] a chemical had been banned solely because it imperiled wildlife." The EPA is now phasing out use of granular carbofuran in the United States.

The EPA registration process now requires tests to detect threats to wildlife. The tests are not perfect, however, and many older pesticides have not had to pass them. Concerned citizens, therefore, will still need to watch for trouble and take action if needed, as they did in Virginia.

Human pesticide poisoning

Many people care about wildlife, but the greatest fears about pesticides center on human health. Pesticides have saved lives by killing pests that spread disease and by improving food supplies. They have also poisoned people, however. And some environmental and consumer groups think pesticides in food help to cause cancer and other illnesses.

It is hard to judge how many people in the world are poisoned by pesticides each year; according to one recent WHO estimate, a million poisonings and 20,000 deaths occur yearly. Another WHO estimate gave a figure of 25 million poisonings and 220,000 deaths. One reason for this large difference may be that most poisoning cases, especially in the Third

DAN,,,THIS FARMER AND HIS WIFE SAY THEY HAVE BEEN EATING GRAPES WITH PESTICIDES FOR YEARS AND THEY'RE IN PERFECT HEALTH,,,,

World, are not reported. People either cannot reach medical care or do not realize that they have been poisoned by pesticides. It is possible that the first figure refers to reported cases and the second includes estimates of unreported ones.

Some pesticide poisonings occur when people use the chemicals for suicide or murder. Others happen when children find pesticides that their families have not stored safely. Pesticide manufacturers cannot be blamed for these events, but the companies bear some responsibility for poisonings of workers who make or use the chemicals. About 40 percent of accidental pesticide poisonings happen on the job.

Some mass poisonings have occurred in or near plants where pesticides are made. The worst happened in 1984 in Bhopal, India, where a plant owned by Union Carbide, a U.S. firm, made methyl isocyanate, an active ingredient in some pesticides. There was an explosion in the plant, and a cloud of this poisonous chemical was released over a heavily populated area. More than 2,000 people were killed, and about 150,000 were injured.

Death in the Third World

Most workers who are poisoned experience this misfortune as they apply pesticides. Some poisonings happen in developed countries. A 1987 study estimated that 300,000 farmworkers in the United States are poisoned by pesticides each year, for example. Workers are also poisoned in other occupations that use pesticides; employees in water purification plants are an example. Poisonings of workers, especially farmworkers, and their families are most common in the Third World. At least half the poisonings caused by pesticides, and more than half the deaths, happen in Third World countries.

Poisonings are frequent in the Third World for many reasons. For example, pesticide labels often lack safety warnings or are not printed in a language local people can read. (Many Third World people cannot read at all.) Some pesticide companies also sell Third World countries pesticides that are not registered in the United States. The companies can do this legally if the purchasing country's government accepts the pesticides. Some pesticides are unregistered because they treat pests not found in the United States. Others, however, have been banned for safety reasons. The U.S. General Accounting Office reported in 1991 that about 25 percent of the pesticides the United States exports are not registered.

Third World farmers and farmworkers are seldom given the training or equipment they need to use pesticides safely. Workers may lack protective clothing, for example. They may have leaky sprayers that drip pesticides onto their skin.

A worker in Bolivia sprays tomato plants with pesticides. Third World countries often lack information on safe handling procedures for chemicals, making pesticide users susceptible to illness or injury.

Other poisonings happen at home. People sometimes mix concentrated pesticide with water or oil. If they store or sell the mixture in bottles that once held drinks, family members are likely to drink the poison by mistake. Some families poison themselves by storing food or water in containers that once held pesticides. Others get sick or die when they eat fish that live in irrigation ditches, since pesticides from farmers' fields wash into the ditches.

Pesticide companies could prevent some of these problems. They could make sure that pesticide labels have safety information in the languages of the countries where the chemicals are sold. Better yet, they could use pictures. (Some already do this.) They could put safety warnings in advertisements. They could make sure that the reasons for a pesticide ban in one country are clear to potential buyers in another country. They could also stop selling banned pesticides.

Pesticides in food

Pesticide residues in food have also raised health concerns. Such residues have never been proven to cause death in the United

States. The question of illness is harder to answer, however. This is most true for diseases like cancer that take years to develop and have unclear causes.

Pesticide scares seem to grab headlines every few years, as in the case of the compound called Alar, or daminozide, in 1989. Alar was really a growth regulator, not a pesticide. Growers used it to make apples redder and get them to ripen at the same time, to make picking easier. The concerns raised by the use of Alar, however, were like those raised over pesticides.

An environmental group called the Natural Resources Defense Council (NRDC) started the fuss. It published a report saying that twenty-three pesticides and other chemicals in food presented an "intolerable risk" to health, especially that of children. The report said that Alar was the worst threat because once inside the body, it breaks down into another chemical, which causes cancer in rats. The NRDC report claimed that up to 273 children in every million would develop cancer because of exposure to this chemical, called UDMH. The environmentalists demanded that the EPA ban Alar at once.

A terrifying prospect

The prospect of children getting cancer from apples was terrifying. Newspapers and TV shows carried NRDC's story. Actress Meryl Streep begged for the banning of Alar. Some parents and schools stopped buying apples and apple products. Apple growers lost up to $150 million in sales. The EPA banned Alar within a few months.

Perhaps the worst thing about the Alar panic was that it seems to have been unnecessary. The EPA estimated that if the growth-regulating chemical were used as intended, at most forty-five people in a million would get cancer because of UDMH. This figure was much lower than NRDC's, but it was still above the agency's standard of "negligible risk." (The EPA defines "negligible risk" as up to one more cancer case per million people than would occur anyway from other causes.) The agency therefore was already phasing out Alar. Most growers had stopped using it. At the time of the NRDC report, the EPA said that, at most, 15 percent of apples were sprayed with Alar. Thus, Alar probably could have been banned without the public panic that made growers lose so much money. Many

Actress Meryl Streep talks with senators John Warner and Steve Symms during Senate subcommittee hearings about the safety of Alar. After much panic, Alar was deemed an acceptable pesticide by the EPA.

other pesticide scares also seem to produce more panic than is really justified.

Setting tolerances

How good is the EPA's way of deciding how much of an added chemical to allow in food? This question is at the heart of the dispute about Alar and other food chemicals, including pesticides. Some groups think the agency's methods keep food quite safe. Others strongly disagree. They think the EPA should do more tests and set stricter limits.

Chemicals are not tested on humans because this practice is not ethical. The EPA therefore sets tolerances, or permitted levels, of chemicals in food by testing laboratory animals such as rats. EPA scientists feed different amounts, or doses, of a chemical to different groups of rats. They monitor the rats carefully, looking for signs of illness. When the rats die, the scientists study their body organs.

These tests tell scientists the largest amount of chemical (per unit of body weight) that seems to cause no harm to the rats. This is the No Observed Effect Level (NOEL). To be on the safe side, the scientists most often divide the NOEL by 100. The result is sometimes called the Acceptable Daily Intake (ADI).

To decide how much of the chemical will be allowed in a certain kind of food, the scientists estimate how much of that food an average person eats in a lifetime. They may do this by using surveys of eating habits, for example. They try to set a tolerance that ensures that the average person will not consume more than the ADI for that chemical, considering all the foods in which it might be found.

The EPA sets tolerances because of the belief that "the dose makes the poison." This means that for any substance, even a poisonous one, there is some amount too small to cause harm. There is good reason to think this is true for most chemicals. The EPA tries to find this amount and make sure people are not likely to consume more than that.

The rules change for cancer

EPA scientists also do tests to find out whether a given chemical can cause cancer in rats or mice. They give the animals the "maximum tolerated dose" of the chemical. This is the greatest amount the animals can take in and still live a normal length of time. The scientists do not expect people to be exposed to such large doses. Rather, they want to give test animals doses large enough to ensure that if the chemical does cause cancer, this property will show up in the small number of animals designated for testing.

Anything that can cause cancer is called a carcinogen. If a chemical proves to be a carcinogen, its use in food is prohibited by the Delaney Clause, a 1958 amendment to the Food, Drug,

and Cosmetic Act of 1938. The Delaney Clause states that "no [food] additive shall be deemed safe if it is found to induce [cause] cancer when ingested [consumed] by man or animal."

In cancer, certain body cells multiply wildly. The process seems to start when one or more genes (units of inherited information) that control cell growth are damaged or destroyed. Factors in the environment sometimes cause the damage. High doses of X rays can do it, for example. Some cancers can start from damage to a single gene in a single cell. Thus it is possible—though by no means sure—that just one molecule of a chemical carcinogen could cause cancer if it damaged the right gene. If this is true, no dose of a carcinogen, no matter how small, can be safe. That is the thinking behind the Delaney Clause.

Farm pesticides are often sprayed from the air. Although the EPA performs tests to set a tolerance level of exposure toward such pesticides, some people fear that such tests are flawed.

Many cancers, however, do not develop until several genes have been damaged. The genes may be harmed at different times. Thus damage from different carcinogens can accumulate. Even though the health risk from any one carcinogen exposure is small, the risks may add up.

Not everyone thinks the Delaney Clause's "no tolerance" policy makes sense. The law's foes call it "outdated" at best. They point out that scientists can now detect much smaller amounts of chemicals than they could in 1958, when the legislation was passed. Tests for identifying carcinogens are also more sensitive. Up to half of all chemicals now tested cause cancer at some dose. Critics say that getting rid of tiny amounts of all these chemicals is neither practical nor necessary. Until a 1992 court decision forced the EPA to enforce the Delaney Clause, the agency often used the "negligible risk" standard instead.

Rats + risk = uncertainty

For now, the EPA's tests are the best way to determine the safety of chemicals. Advocates on both sides of the food safety debate agree, however, that testing high doses of chemicals on rats is a poor way to predict the effects of low doses on people. Rats are like humans in some ways but not in others. High doses may also have effects that low doses would not produce. A massive amount of any substance—including those not usually thought of as harmful—may damage animals' bodies, perhaps even causing cancer. Salt and sugar can cause cancer in animals if given in high enough doses.

Both sides in the food safety debate also agree that a statement like "such-and-such a dose of Alar will cause forty-five extra cancer cases in every million people" is not nearly as precise as it sounds. Scientists cannot really tell how many cancers—if any—a chemical will cause. Statements like these are statements of *risk*. Risk is the chance that some harmful event will happen. It is written as a ratio or a fraction. The fraction is often stated as follows: "A person's lifetime chance of getting cancer from chemical A at such-and-such an average daily dose is 1 in 100,000." Put another way, the statement might read, "One in every 100,000 people exposed to such-and-such a daily dose of chemical A will get cancer." Or again, "Out of a population of 100,000 people exposed to such-and-such a daily dose of chemical A, the fraction that will get cancer is 1/100,000."

The calculation of risk is complicated. It involves many assumptions about what is likely to happen under different conditions. Some of these assumptions may be wrong. Assumptions about what happens to adults may not apply to children, for instance. The estimates used in the calculations also may not be precise. For example, different surveys might give different estimates for the amount of certain foods that people eat in a lifetime. In short, statements of risk are guesses. They do not prove that, say, forty-five real people out of a million will get cancer because of exposure to some chemical.

Comparing risks

As with animal tests, however, risk statements are all we have. We have to use them in deciding which risks to try to reduce. One way to make such decisions is to compare different risks. For example, the EPA says that the risk of getting cancer from Alar is forty-five in a million. Studies have shown that the risk of dying in a car accident is 1 in 4,000. A person who starts smoking at age fifteen and smokes a pack of cigarettes a day will have a risk of dying from lung cancer of 1 in 800. (Carcinogens in cigarette smoke often cause lung cancer.) Bruce Ames, a scientist at the University of California, Berkeley, claims that people run a higher health risk from natural pesticides in many plant foods than they do from pesticides added to those same foods. Thus, compared to many health risks, those from pesticides in food seem small.

An unfamiliar risk

Most people, however, judge risks more by feelings than by mathematics. A small risk of one kind may *feel* worse than a large risk of another kind. Robert Scheuplein, a scientist with the U.S. Food and Drug Administration (FDA), says people are most likely to feel angry about risks that seem "dread, fatal, unfamiliar, uncontrollable by the individual, unfair, involuntary, and potentially catastrophic." Thus, most people accept the fairly high risk of dying in a car accident because cars are familiar. Pesticides, however, seem unfamiliar and "unnatural." People choose to ride in cars, but they do not ask to have pesticides put in their food. People also dread cancer, which pesticides are said to cause, more than most diseases. Because of these feelings, as the Alar scare showed, many people object strongly to risks from pesticides even when these risks are slight. As one writer in the *Nation* put it, "Maybe [the consumer] . . . is at greater risk of getting hit by a car than of contracting cancer from pesticide-laden broccoli. So what?" Television often makes matters worse by showing dramatic images and stressing one side of an issue.

Even when a risk is comparatively small, it should not necessarily be ignored. Sometimes getting rid of the cause of a small health risk makes more sense than removing the cause of a larger risk. No one recommends avoiding fruits and vegetables because they contain natural pesticides, for example. These foods are vital in a healthy diet. Many even contain substances that fight cancer. The benefits of fruits and vegetables clearly outweigh their risks. Some people feel this is true of artificial pesticides, too. Others disagree. They see no reason to accept any risks from these chemicals.

Debates continue

Debates about the health risks of pesticides in foods are sure to continue. Scientists still cannot say exactly how cancer starts. They know little about the effect of tiny doses of chemicals on the body. Without sure knowledge, people are likely to go on splitting into two camps. One holds pes-

Farmworkers ride on a cart full of just-picked apples. Most people believe the health benefits of eating fruits and vegetables far outweigh the small risk of ingesting pesticides.

ticides innocent until proven guilty. The other does just the opposite.

The best we can do is try to use what we do know rather than letting our feelings rule us. We can try to keep risks in perspective by comparing them with other risks and with benefits. We can also remember that money and time are limited. We cannot get rid of all health risks. We must therefore choose which risks we will try to reduce. We can try to make the choices that will protect our health most effectively.

5

Alternatives to Pesticides

RACHEL CARSON SAID that in using pesticides, people were trying to control nature. If so, nature proved to be much harder to control than people thought. Instead of giving in, it has turned our weapons against us. Because of the way natural processes react to them, pesticides often make pest problems worse instead of better. These reactions may provide a better reason than health fears for trying to use fewer pesticides.

Pests fight back

One natural reaction is the development of pest resistance. Resistance results from evolution, the changes in living things that occur because of changes in, for example, their environment. Suppose a field of potatoes is sprayed with DDT to kill potato beetles. Most of the beetles die, but a few escape. Some are just lucky (the spray missed them), but others, by chance, have a way of fighting off the poison. Perhaps their bodies break it down before it harms them.

The beetles that survive will have offspring, which may inherit the component in the parents' bodies that protected them from DDT. Repeated

(Opposite page) Using biology to control pests has become a popular technique. Here, a lacewing larva feeds on destructive aphids.

71

spraying will kill all the beetles except those that have genetic (inherited) resistance.

Most pesticides also kill natural enemies of pests. With their enemies gone, resistant pests often multiply to greater numbers than existed before pesticide treatment. Killing enemies can also "create" new pests. That happened with an insect called the brown planthopper. This insect had always lived in Asian rice fields, especially in India, and in the islands of Malaysia, Indonesia, and the Philippines. It became a major pest, however, only after the Green Revolution of the 1970s brought heavy pesticide use. Pesticides killed the planthopper's enemies and let it multiply. By the late 1970s, the brown planthopper was considered the worst rice pest in Asia.

The pesticide treadmill

The greater the quantity of pesticide used, the more quickly these problems appear. If the response to the new problems is more spraying, the problems will become worse still. This vicious circle has been called the "pesticide treadmill." Losses grow as pest damage and money spent on pesticides increase.

Resistance and related problems have caused trouble everywhere pesticides have been used. David Pimentel, a Cornell University scientist, estimates that pest controllers in the United States spend $1.4 billion a year just to fight resistant insects. Resistance problems have been worst, however, in the Third World. Resistance helped to undo most of the lifesaving work of WHO's malaria program, for example. Mosquitoes began developing resistance to DDT in the late 1960s. Heavy use of pesticides in farming probably speeded up the process. The number of malaria cases then started to rise. The number of new cases worldwide increased 230 percent between 1972 and 1976.

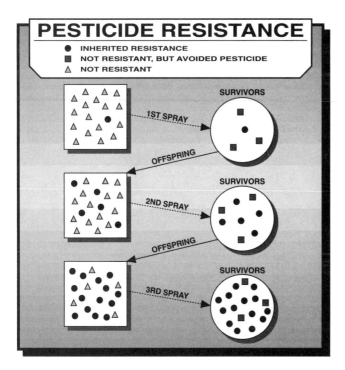

PESTICIDE RESISTANCE

● INHERITED RESISTANCE
■ NOT RESISTANT, BUT AVOIDED PESTICIDE
△ NOT RESISTANT

Today more than five hundred insect species can resist one or more pesticides. About fifty-five species of weeds and one hundred species of microorganisms that cause plant diseases are also resistant. Seventeen insect species resist all pesticides.

The only way to slow development of pesticide resistance is to use the chemicals less heavily and less often. This strategy results in the survival of more pests. These nonresistant pests breed with the resistant ones and pass on their own genetic information. The pest population then contains both resistant and nonresistant members. A completely resistant population does not build up. This means that when really needed, pesticides will still be able to control pests.

The enemy of my enemy is my friend

It is possible to use less pesticide and still control pests because there are good pest control methods that do not use chemicals. Some pest controllers use only these methods. Because these forms of pest control are complex and several are often used together, pests are less likely to develop resistance to them.

Probably the most popular alternative to chemical pesticides is biological control, which puts nature on our side in the pest war. In nature, different kinds of plants and animals attack or compete with each other. As a result, no one kind takes over. The old Arab proverb "The enemy of my enemy is my friend" could be a slogan for biological control.

Looking for a few good bugs

Most biological control uses insects to control other insects. "It's just like cats controlling mice, except these animals are smaller and have more legs," says Jake Blehm, head of the Association of Natural Biocontrol Producers. People can buy some of these insects from companies that raise them. Others are already present in farms or gardens.

Some "good bugs" are predators. Ladybugs, the best known of these six-legged tigers, devour

The natural predator qualities of the praying mantis make it a perfect attacker for many common pests.

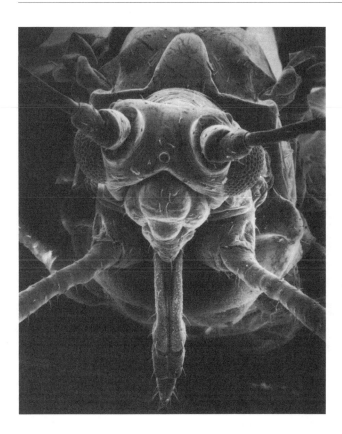

A scanning electron micrograph shows the head of an aphid at two hundred times its natural size. Clearly featured is the aphid's proboscis—a slender trunk with which it penetrates plant tissue.

aphids, mealybugs, scale insects, and other pests. Other useful predators include lacewing larvae (sometimes called "aphid lions") and praying mantises.

Parasites can be even more effective pest controllers. Insect parasites lay their eggs in the bodies or eggs of other insects. When the eggs hatch, the parasite larvae use the other insects' bodies as food. The most common pest control parasites are tiny, stingless wasps. Most lay their eggs in caterpillars.

Insects can also control weeds. In the early 1990s, for example, an insect called the hairy weevil was brought from Greece to the United States to control yellow star thistles. These weeds ruin pasture land because they have sharp thorns and a poison that makes horses sick.

Before being released in the United States, weed-eating flea beetles are caged with different crops and plants to ensure that they will not destroy non target plants.

Many living things used in biological control, like the hairy weevil, are imported. This makes sense because many pests also come from other countries. They become pests in their new home partly because they have no enemies there. Scientists look for the enemies that kept the pest's numbers down in its old home. Then they try to restore nature's balance by bringing the enemies to the new home, too.

More than 150 kinds of insect pests have been controlled by imported insects. Imported insects also control at least 30 kinds of weeds worldwide. A 1982 study reported that "foreign" insects saved farmers nearly a billion dollars a year in California alone.

Importing must be done with caution, however. Some living things imported for biological control become pests themselves. If scientists plan to import a living thing, they first study it in sealed greenhouses. They see what useful plants or animals it might harm. Only if it seems harmless is it allowed outside. Then it is tested further before being released. Like pesticides, imported living things must gain government approval before being used in this country.

If a pest does not come from another country, its enemies are likely to be nearby. Sometimes the enemies can be brought into action just by avoiding pesticides that harm them. Growing plants that "good" insects like to live in can also help. Some garden supply stores sell seed mixtures of fennel, clover, and other plants helpful insects like.

The ideal insecticide?

Some living things used in biological control are too small to see without a microscope. Most are bacteria that cause insect diseases. Today's most widely used biological control bacterium is *Bacillus thuringiensis*, or Bt for short. It most often lives in soil. It got its name in 1911, when scientists found it in the German town of Thuringen. Different Bt species live all over the world.

Each of the thousands of types of Bt infects just one group of closely related insects. One kind of Bt often used in biological control infects caterpillars. Another infects mosquito larvae. Scientists are always looking for new types of Bt that attack other pest insects.

Under harsh conditions such as drought, Bt bacteria form bodies called spores. A spore puts a bacterium's genes in a protective coat. Each spore also carries a crystal. If the target insect eats the spore, the spore wall dissolves, releasing the crystal. Chemicals in the crystal make holes in the insect's gut. The bacteria then spread through the insect's body and kill it.

Although Bt was first used commercially in 1938, it was soon overshadowed by DDT and other pesticides. In the late 1960s, when people began to question the safety of chemicals, Bt came back into use. Sprays and dusts containing Bt as the active ingredient can now be bought at many garden supply stores.

In some ways, Bt is the ideal insecticide. It is cheap. It does not harm plants, fish, birds, or mammals. Each type kills only a few kinds of insects. So far, few insects are resistant to it.

Bt does have some drawbacks, however. The main one is that sunlight kills its spores just a few days after the insecticide has been sprayed on. This means that the spray must be reapplied

A geneticist sprays a Bt solution on tomato plants to determine its toxicity to the Colorado potato beetle. Bt pesticides are preferable today because they use bacteria to destroy insects.

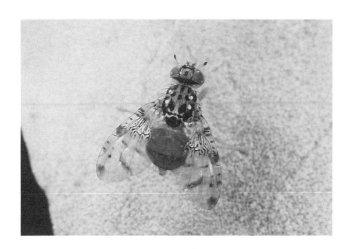

Medflies are controlled by harvesting crops of males and making them sterile. When these sterile medflies mate, they cannot produce offspring.

often. Bt also takes several days to kill insects, although they stop feeding on the plants they inhabit in a day or so. Scientists are trying to make Bt act faster and last longer.

Making it hard to find a mate

Other alternatives to pesticides turn insects' urge to mate against them. In one technique, millions of male pest insects are raised in a laboratory. They are made sterile (unable to produce young) by radiation and then released. Males are used because among insects, males often mate many times. Most females mate just once. If a female mates with a sterile male, she will not have offspring.

The technique of flooding an area with sterile males was used in the 1950s to control the screwworm fly, a livestock pest, in the southern United States. In the early 1980s it was used, along with malathion spraying, to control Mediterranean fruit flies (medflies) in Florida. It works best when pest numbers are not too large and pests can be kept from moving back into an area. (The screwworm fly population rose again a few years after the treatment because new flies came in from Mexico.)

Scientists are experimenting with pheromones to lure parasites and predators, such as the spined soldier bug, to areas where they are likely to find pests on which to feed.

U.S. Department of Agriculture officials load an airplane with a box containing millions of infertile medflies. The medflies will be dropped over a fifty-square-mile area of Miami.

Agriculture department technicians check traps that have been baited with small amounts of pheromones.

Another control technique disturbs pest insects' sex lives in a different way. Many insects make chemicals called pheromones, which send messages to other insects when released into the air. Some female insects send out pheromones when they are ready to mate. When a male senses the pheromone from a female of his species, he follows the chemical "trail" to the female. If a tiny amount of mating pheromone is put in a trap, male pest insects can be lured from miles away. Clouds of artificial pheromones released into the air can confuse the insects so badly that they cannot find mates.

Old techniques with new twists

Some alternatives to pesticides are methods people have used for thousands of years. Often they are now applied with new, high-tech twists. Physical controls, the oldest methods of all, still work well. Clear plastic covers over plants let in sunlight, air, and water but keep insects out. Black covers keep weeds from growing before crop seeds come up. Traps baited with food, pheromones, or ultraviolet ("black") light catch insects. Some farmers suck insects off crops with a giant vacuum cleaner called a Bug Vac.

Farmers are also rediscovering cultural controls such as crop rotation. Alternating crops of corn, oats, and soybeans prevents problems with corn rootworms, for example. Using sorghum as part of crop rotation discourages weeds. The sorghum plants give out a chemical that stops weed growth.

Putting certain plants near crops controls some pests. One kind of weed related to cabbage, planted next to corn, emits a chemical that kills corn-destroying worms and fungi. Other plants act as "trap crops." For example, rows of alfalfa plants in cotton fields can be traps for lygus bugs, which like alfalfa even better than they like

Some farmers use a Bug Vac, a huge vacuum cleaner, to suck insects off their plants.

cotton. Once the bugs have gathered in the alfalfa, they can be killed with small amounts of insecticide.

Keeping clean helps prevent many human diseases. It helps prevent pest attacks on farms, too. Some farmers are turning away from no-till agriculture and from leaving farm waste on the ground because these habits encourage pest insects. Insects or their eggs often survive the winter in soil or stalks of dead plants. The insects can be killed, however, if the plants are removed and the soil is broken up by plowing.

Scientists use another ancient method, plant breeding, to make new surprises for pests. For example, Cornell University and the International Potato Center in Lima, Peru, are crossbreeding edible potatoes with certain wild potatoes from Bolivia. The Bolivian potatoes are not good to eat, but the leaves and stems of the plants are covered with sticky hairs that trap small insects such as aphids. The hairs give larger insects, such as potato beetles, indigestion when the insects eat the plants. If an edible "hairy potato" could be produced, it would need little or no pesticide because it would provide its own defense.

Genetic engineering

Changing inherited information by breeding is a slow process, however, and it works only between closely related types of living things. Instead of using breeding, scientists are learning how to put genes from any living thing directly into other living things. This new science, genetic engineering, offers new hopes for pest control.

One project involves putting genes for Bt poisons into crop plants. This would solve the problem of Bt spores being killed by sunlight. Cotton plants with Bt genes should be on sale in a few years. Bt-containing potatoes, tomatoes, and other crops no doubt will soon follow.

Some scientists fear that exposing pests to constant high doses of Bt poison in plants will bring on resistance, just as happened with artificial pesticides. The best way to avoid this may be to mix plants without Bt genes among those that have the genes. Insects not resistant to the Bt poisons can survive on these plants. They will breed with any resistant insects. This should keep resistant populations from developing. "Bt crops will last three to four years if we use the product poorly, and thirty to forty years if we use the product well," says Ed Bruggemann, a scientist with the National Audubon Society.

A more controversial use of genetic engineering is the creation of crop plants that resist herbicides. This is the purpose of 29 percent of genetically engineered crops being tested in America today. Several large firms that make herbicides, such as Monsanto Corporation, are trying to produce such plants. Each company is making plants that resist its own brand of herbicide. If crop plants were resistant, farmers could apply larger doses of weed killers without harming the valuable plants.

Environmentalists say this form of genetic engineering will tie farmers to the pesticide treadmill more closely than ever. There is also some

An entomologist compares an insect-ravaged cotton leaf with one that has been genetically engineered to improve its natural resistance to insects.

The cotton boll on the right was protected by a gene for Bt, while the other bolls have been damaged by pests. Some question the safety of manipulating the genes of plants.

danger that wind could carry pollen that contains resistance genes from crop plants to wild relatives that are weeds. The result could be resistant "superweeds." Experiments have shown that engineered genes in pollen can spread much farther than scientists suspected.

Is genetic engineering safe?

Some people wonder whether genetic engineering for any purpose is safe. They fear that genes that were harmless in their natural places may change or mutate in dangerous ways after they are put into other living things. Genes put into harmless bacteria might change in a way that empowers the bacteria to cause disease, for example. Supporters of genetic engineering think dangerous mutations are unlikely to happen. They believe such fears are just another example of worry about small risks that comes from the unfamiliar.

No one really knows what the dangers of this new technology are. Nearly everyone wants to avoid the mistakes people made in using pesticides widely before they understood the chemicals' effects. At the very least, genetically engineered living things should be carefully studied in laboratories before release.

Drawbacks of nonchemical control

Biological control and other alternatives to pesticides are not perfect. Like pesticides, they can backfire if not used carefully. Living things imported to control pests may become pests themselves, for example.

Nonchemical methods also do not always work. For each biological control success story

Experiments with genetic engineering could accidentally result in the creation of a "superweed" that resists herbicides. Its other troubling features could include large, unsightly leaves and stems, sharp thorns, and long, strong roots.

there have been many failures. Imported pest control agents often die out because the new environment is too different from their old one. "A lot of organisms give good results under controlled conditions, but they don't work out in practice," says William Connick, a chemist with the USDA.

Even when nonchemical methods do succeed, they are not as fast acting or dramatic in their effects as chemicals. They often need days, weeks, or even whole seasons to take effect. They also do not produce the comforting sight of piles of dead insects. Jack Coulson of the USDA notes, "Natural enemies don't provide the immediate control growers want."

Time for a change?

The percentage of farmers and other pest controllers that use only nonchemical methods is still

In an attempt to avoid using pesticides, a farmer uses insect traps on his apple trees. If trapping fails to control insect pests, he will have to resort to pesticides.

quite small. It is growing, however. Some people who give up pesticides are trying to reverse losses caused by the pesticide treadmill. Others are tired of the regulations that surround pesticide use. Some worry about what pesticides may do to the environment and human health. Others are simply reacting to the worry expressed by consumers. They know that some shoppers will pay higher prices for foods grown without pesticides. Along with the money saved by not buying chemicals, these high prices can offset any added losses from pests and make pesticide-free farming profitable.

6

The Future
of Pesticides

PESTS ARE STILL A THREAT to human health and food supplies. Some studies estimate that 35 percent of the world's crops are lost to pests each year. Malaria, carried by mosquitoes, attacks about 100 million people yearly. And about eleven potential new pests come into the United States each year. "We get a serious new pest every three years on the average," says Jack Coulson of the USDA.

New losses, new dangers

Pesticides seemed to promise victory in human efforts to defeat pests. They have brought no such thing. David Pimentel of Cornell says that Americans use ten times as much pesticide as they did in 1945. Losses of farm crops to pests, however, have doubled since that year. Part of the reason is the rise of farming techniques that encourage pests, such as monoculture. Part is due to pesticide resistance and related problems.

People are still worried about pesticides' effects on health and the environment. Indeed, new reasons for concern have surfaced. One involves Rachel Carson's old foes, the organochlorines.

(Opposite page) Entomologists release canisters of parasitic wasps to control insects on crops in Alabama.

"What a day! . . . I must have spread malaria across half the country."

Residues of these pesticides are still found all over the world. Scientists have recently shown that they are related to estrogen, a normal chemical in female mammals that helps to make them female. The organochlorines and some other chemical pollutants seem to have effects like those of estrogen in humans and animals. Some male animals exposed to high amounts of these chemicals develop reproductive systems that look like those of females. The chemicals may be involved in the recent rise in breast cancer in women and cancer of the testicles in men. They may also be connected with drops in male fertility and in average number of sperm during the last fifty years. Some studies have found that men who have eaten pesticide-free food for years have sperm counts much higher than the present average.

New pesticides

Some scientists are trying to solve the problems of pests and pesticides by making new kinds of pesticides. Some of these may be less harmful to people and wildlife than older pesticides. The less toxic substances are related to chemicals found only in insects' bodies. These natural chemicals serve such purposes as the control of molting (shedding of an insect's hard skin) or the change from wormlike larvae to hard-bodied adults. Some new pesticides interfere with these chemicals. Others are like the chemicals but are given at the wrong time in the insect species' life cycle. Both kinds either make insects mature too fast or keep them from maturing at all. Either way, the insects die without having young.

Other scientists are studying natural insecticides made by plants. Some of the most interesting of these pesticides come from a tree called the neem. Neem trees grow in Africa, India, and Asia, where people have used them for many purposes, including pest control, for centuries. For example, they have put neem leaves in grain bins to keep weevils out.

Some compounds in neem seeds prevent reproduction by disrupting insects' natural growth process. They repel or kill more than two hundred pest insect species. They do not seem to harm mice, birds, or useful insects. A 1992 National Research Council report claimed that "the [neem] tree is probably the single best source of biopesticides [pesticides based on chemicals in living things] around." Pesticides made from the neem can be bought in many states.

It is not clear, however, that new pesticides will work better than the old ones. It would seem

Neem trees possess natural pesticidal qualities. They are capable of repelling or killing more than two hundred insect species.

impossible for insects to resist pesticides related to their own body chemicals, but in some cases it has happened. Such pesticides might also harm useful insects as well as pests.

Are pesticides a good investment?

What is the future of pesticides? Whether people will increase their reliance on chemicals for solving pest problems or turn more to non-chemical tools will depend greatly on economics. Farmers care about the environment, but they also care about making a living. Shoppers worry about their health, but they also worry about how much money they spend on food.

Pesticide supporters say pesticides are a good investment. They pay back about $4 in crop yield for every dollar spent. Critics of pesticides point out, however, that this figure may not include the indirect costs of using pesticides. These include costs of health care and lost work time for poisoned workers. Damage to wildlife has costs, too. Indirect costs of pesticide use in America amount to between $1 billion and $8 billion a year.

Even with indirect costs included, the benefits of pesticide use often outweigh their costs, but sometimes not by much. There are also instances of costs outweighing benefits. The International Rice Research Institute in the Philippines says that when health costs are taken into account, the costs of using pesticides on rice (a major Third World food crop) outweigh the benefits. Also, even when pesticides are a good investment, nonchemical methods may be a better one. Some studies say biological control returns $25 or more for each dollar spent.

What would happen without pesticides?

Scientists have also estimated the costs of *not* using pesticides. Some say that if all pesticide use stopped, worldwide crop losses to pests would rise 10 percent or more. Others say the rise would be only 5 percent. Losses would probably be highest in the Third World.

Indirect costs of not using pesticides include more money spent on labor and food processing. More land would have to be farmed to grow the same amount of usable food. This would leave less for open space and wildlife habitat.

If farmers lose more of their crops to pests, they will charge more for what they do raise. Studies suggest that a ban on all pesticides would raise average food prices by 5 to 12 percent. Losses and price changes would be greater for some crops than others. For example, the National Agricultural Chemicals Association

These voracious caterpillars can consume and destroy grape leaves at a ferocious pace. The destruction caused by such pests cannot be allowed to progress, but pesticides are not the only way to stop it.

claims that without pesticides, prices for fruits and vegetables would rise 50 percent.

Poor families would suffer the most from increased food prices. If costs of fruits and vegetables rise, such families might not buy them. Yet these foods are vital to a good diet, and if families do without them, their health may suffer.

Reducing pesticide use

Few people seek a complete ban of pesticides. Rachel Carson did not. Most environmental groups do not. What most want is a *reduction* in pesticide use. This most likely could be achieved at much less cost than a total ban. A recent study by David Pimentel claims that U.S. pesticide use could be cut by 50 percent with no overall loss in crop yields. Food prices would rise just 0.6 percent. "The environmental and public-health benefits of reducing pesticide use would more than balance this cost and actually provide net benefits to the economy," Pimentel says. Again, however, some crops would be hurt more than others.

Most farmers who have tried cutting pesticide use have not suffered. In a 1989 survey of a thousand farmers conducted by *New Farm* magazine, only 4 percent said their net income had gone down after they reduced pesticides; 32 percent said their income had gone up. In the same year a report by the National Research Council said that most farmers who apply few or no pesticides have crop yields as great as those who use pesticides. Even when the yield is a little lower, the profit may be as great or greater. This is so because the costs are less.

A middle ground

The most likely future of pesticides is as part of pest control programs that use these substances sparingly and combine them with nonchemical methods. The idea behind such programs is called

These California vineyards are run organically, free of pesticides. Many farmers who grow their crops without pesticides say that they suffer no loss in profits.

Integrated Pest Management (IPM). IPM is a middle ground between extensive pesticide use and no use of pesticides.

Perhaps the best reason for using IPM is that it decreases the chance of pest resistance. Resistance is unlikely to develop in an IPM program because such a program always includes several pest control methods. No one method is used heavily enough to encourage resistance. A pest that becomes resistant to one kind of treatment can still be controlled by other methods.

An IPM program does not try to kill all pests. Instead, it aims to keep losses from pests below the level of "economic injury." This is the level at which the value of lost crops or other goods starts to be greater than the cost of controlling the pests. Some parts of an IPM program, such as native natural enemies and cultural techniques, are used all the time. Others, including pesticides, are used only when pest losses reach an "economic damage threshold." This level is set lower than the economic injury level because most pest control methods need time to take effect.

Designing an IPM program

The best IPM programs are designed by IPM experts working with the people who will use the programs. The designers start by studying the ecosystem in which a program will be used. This may be a farm, a forest, an office building, or a home. The designers determine what kinds of pests are there and how many. They learn what the pests eat and how much damage they do. They see what other living things, including enemies of pests, are in the area. They study physical factors such as weather and soil. People are part of the ecosystem, too. IPM designers therefore look at economic and social factors that might affect the program.

The designers of an IPM program can choose among all the pest control methods ever invented, from sticky traps to genetic engineering. Their choices will depend on the situation. Designers try to pick groups of methods that will keep pests below the economic damage threshold with the least cost and risk to environment and health. If the situation changes, so does the program.

IPM in action

One of the first IPM programs was developed to control an aphid that ate alfalfa, a kind of hay used for cattle food. The spotted alfalfa aphid was accidentally brought to New Mexico in 1954 and had spread through the Southwest by 1955. In 1957 damage from the aphid infestation cost California alfalfa growers $10.6 million.

At first farmers sprayed their crops with parathion and malathion. This treatment killed some aphids, but it killed insects that ate aphids as well. Some researchers thought it also might leave residues in the milk of cows that ate the alfalfa. Farmers therefore needed a better way to control the aphids.

Together, with the help of scientists, the California farmers began an integrated program to eliminate the aphids. Scientists used advanced plant breeding techniques to develop types of alfalfa that could resist the aphids, and farmers planted only these types. Farmers also stopped using pesticides, giving ladybugs and other predators a chance to attack the aphids. Three wasp parasites that preyed on the aphids in their European home were also released in California. Farmers learned to take away the aphids' shelter by cutting the alfalfa so that no plant parts were left on the ground.

The farmers figured out how many aphids had to be present to cause significant losses in their crop. When numbers passed this level, the farmers used pesticides. They chose chemicals that made the alfalfa plants poisonous to the aphids but did not harm their natural enemies. Within a year, this mix of methods reduced aphid damage in California from $10.6 million to $1.7 million.

More than 50 percent of California farmers practice some form of IPM today. For example, the Robert Mondavi Winery in northern California uses special plows rather than herbicides to kill weeds around most of its grapevines. Winery workers also set up perches and nesting boxes to attract hawks and owls. These birds eat gophers, which dig up the soil around the vines. Workers plant oak and buckeye trees around the edges of the vineyards. The trees and nearby brush provide hiding places for coyotes and bobcats, which kill the jackrabbits that are another pest.

A parasitic wasp lays her eggs in a tobacco budworm. Such parasites have been very useful in controlling harmful insects.

A ladybug consumes an aphid. While pesticides kill harmful insects, they also kill useful ones, such as the ladybug.

IPM can be used wherever pests are a problem. For example, Albert Greene, the national IPM coordinator for the U.S. General Services Administration, organizes IPM programs in federal government buildings nationwide. He points out that such programs have as much to do with people as with pests. They include making sure people put all food waste in sealed containers, for instance. To prevent cockroach problems, Greene recommends caulking (sealing) cracks around plumbing, where the insects can live. If roaches do appear, technicians use backpack vacuums to suck up both the bugs and the food scraps they feed on. When roach populations are heavy, controllers put down bait mixed with boric acid. Used in this way, boric acid kills many species of insects but does not harm people.

IPM in the Third World

Some IPM programs sound so complex that pest controllers might need computers to keep track of them. IPM might thus seem impossible to use in the Third World, where many people cannot even read. But, says Ray Smith, an expert in use of IPM in developing countries, IPM is really just "traditional agriculture with a little bit of sophistication added." There is no reason Third World farmers cannot use it.

Indeed, many Third World farmers are finding that IPM offers an escape from the pesticide treadmill. Unlike the Green Revolution approach to farming, IPM does not need expensive imported chemicals and machines. For the most part it uses tools found on the farm or nearby. Working with advisers, farmers learn to design their own programs and carry them out. Once the programs are running, the farmers need the advisers only in emergencies.

Success in Indonesia

One of the most successful Third World IPM programs is operating in Indonesia, a string of islands west of Southeast Asia. Like other parts of Asia, Indonesia suffered when the brown planthopper became an important rice pest in the early 1980s. In 1986 Indonesian planthoppers ruined enough rice to have fed three million people.

The Indonesian government had been paying part of the costs of farmers' pesticides. In 1986 it instead banned fifty-seven of the sixty-three pesticides farmers had been using and set up a national IPM program with some of the money it had been spending on pesticides. The United Nations Food and Agriculture Organization (FAO) organized the program. The U.S. Agency for International Development and the World Bank helped pay for it.

FAO experts began teaching Indonesia's two-and-a-half million farmers how to use the program. Some of these lessons were taught in field schools. Local actors presented others in traditional village theaters.

The farmers learned to look at their rice paddies as an ecosystem. They learned how to

recognize planthoppers and their natural enemies, including wolf spiders. Besides eating rice plants, the planthoppers carry a disease that attacks the plants. The farmers learned how to tell this disease from other rice diseases. They also learned to predict the number of planthoppers that would cause significant damage to their crop. Only if the farmers saw more than this number would they use pesticides.

The Indonesian farmers worked together to reduce planthopper damage. For example, they planted a small amount of rice early in the season to attract the insects. The planthoppers that gathered in this "trap crop" could be killed with small amounts of insecticide. The farmers then planted their main crop. After harvest, the farmers all left their fields unplanted for a while. This helped to starve the planthoppers out before the next crop was sown.

Advocates of IPM say these programs can be just as useful in rice paddies in Indonesia and other Third World nations as they can be in developed nations.

Trained by IPM field specialists, farmers in Java identify and count insects and draw graphic representations of the rice ecosystem. Using these techniques, farmers will be able to make more informed decisions about pest control.

Ralph Wright of the EPA calls the Indonesian program the "premier [best] IPM program ever attempted." The FAO says Indonesian rice production has increased at least 10 percent since the program's start. Pesticide use has dropped 50 percent.

Barriers to IPM

In both developed and developing countries, however, IPM remains more talked about than used. One reason for this is lack of government support. IPM programs can be expensive to set up. Programs need to be designed. People need to be taught to use them. Farmers need advisers to call on if things go wrong. Governments or international agencies often must pay the costs of these services, and many Third World governments are not willing or able to do this. Developed countries like the United States have also expressed support for IPM more in words than in money.

Lack of education also prevents IPM from becoming more widespread. Many pest controllers do not know how to design or use IPM programs. Often they are willing to learn, however. In a poll conducted by Iowa State University, 56 percent of the state's farmers said they would reduce pesticide use if more information about ways to do so were available.

Many farmers who have heard about IPM still have doubts about it. Some are leery of the complexity of many IPM programs. Others are afraid IPM will make them lose money, especially during the first year or two. Some do not want or cannot afford to spend the time and effort required to manage a successful IPM program. Some do not want to take part in the cooperative efforts often called for by IPM.

Overcoming farmers' doubts

IPM will not spread until farmers' doubts can be overcome. As Michael Hansen of the Consumers' Union says, "The real test of an IPM system is whether or not farmers will use it." In 1990 only 8 percent of U.S. farmland was managed by IPM.

Resistance to using IPM may be dropping, however. "I am astounded at the recent change in attitude," says Marjorie Hoy of the University of California, Berkeley. "Growers are clamoring for new techniques to raise crops." Dave Dyer of American Farmland Trust thinks the 1990s are "the beginning of the end of the chemical era. Agrichemicals will shift from being the driving force [in farming] to being the helping hand."

If IPM does spread, it may bring more changes than just decreased pesticide use. "IPM is . . .

applied ecology," says Frank Zalom, director of IPM research at the University of California at Davis. IPM users certainly want to preserve food and other property and to make a profit. They do not expect to get rid of all pests, however. If they really understand the thinking behind IPM, they see themselves as part of the web of life rather than its rulers. Such people are likely to show their increased respect for nature in ways that go far beyond pest control.

Users of IPM realize that human competition with other living things is more complex than the common comparison to a war suggests. For one thing, the competition will never have a winner. The process of evolution sees to that. "We will continue to come up with ways to kill [pests], and they will continue to survive, one way or another," says Homer LeBaron, a former researcher with Ciba-Geigy, one of the world's largest pesticide makers.

No simple answers

One of the most important lessons the story of pesticides teaches is that complex problems do not have simple solutions. The quick fix for pest problems that pesticides seemed to promise is a dream that failed. This happened because, as Rachel Carson wrote, "nothing stands alone."

In both nature and human society, any action has many effects. Some may be unexpected and undesired. Unpleasant surprises are most likely when we focus on just a small part of a problem, such as killing a single pest or banning a single pesticide. Trying to wipe out pests with chemicals may kill wildlife as well. It also may help surviving pests become resistant. Trying to remove all, or even most, pesticides without finding other methods of control may drive some farmers out of business. It also may raise food prices to the

point that some people who now eat properly will not be able to afford a healthful diet.

As more and more technology appears in our lives, we must learn to face complex questions like those raised by pesticides. We must try to look at such questions with thought rather than emotion. We must try to use our votes, time, money, and other resources in ways that will do the most good. In making careful decisions, we will be acting like the designers of a good IPM program. We will seek a blend of methods that protects our own interests and also safeguards the world around us.

A healthy-looking mustard and grape crop grows in row after row. Farmers and consumers share a common interest in high-quality produce. Today, such growth does not have to come with a high environmental price.

Appendix

When exploring arguments about pesticides:

1. *Beware of appeals to emotions.* Some words and images make people feel rather than think. Environmentalists may say that pesticides spread a "circle of poison" or present an "intolerable risk" to children. Pesticide supporters may call environmentalists "hysterical" or "ecological terrorists." Public service TV ads present pictures of children dying of cancer or fields being devoured by pests. Commercial advertisements teach people to reach for pesticides without thinking about whether the "pests" really harm them. Look for facts, not feelings.

2. *Consider the source.* Find out where information you read, see, or hear comes from. Do the people providing the information have economic or other ties to one side or the other of the arguments about pesticides? Do they have a strong opinion for or against pesticides? Strong feelings may not mean that someone's facts are incorrect. Such feelings may mean, however, that the person tells only one side of the story.

3. *Get both sides of the story.* Look for opinions and facts on both sides of an argument. (This book lists further reading and groups to contact, to give you a start.) Try also to find a middle view that includes some points from both sides. If you talk or write to people with opinions about pesticides, ask questions.

4. *Examine suggested causes.* People sometimes suggest that because one event happened after another, the first event *caused* the second. Common sense tells you that events can follow each other without being connected. Look for more evidence before deciding that one event caused another. Consider possible causes besides the one suggested. Remember that events can have more than one cause.

5. *Consider good and bad effects.* Events can have many effects. The same event may help some groups and harm others. It may both help and harm the same group. Many events and actions have unexpected effects. When judging an event or action, look for both helpful and harmful effects. Look for effects on different groups. Think about possible effects that are not described.

6. *Beware of numbers.* Numbers look very precise, but they may not be. As explained in Chapter 4, some numbers simply describe the chances that something *might* happen. They do not show how often it *will* happen or even whether it will happen at all. Other numbers are estimates, or guesses, based on some supporting data. In making estimates, people find out what happens in a small sample of cases. They then use this information to help them guess what will be true of a larger group. In doing so, they make certain assumptions about how things will act. Different people may arrive at different estimates for the same thing because they use different samples and different assumptions. Try to find out what samples and assumptions people have used to reach their estimates.

7. *Look for the big picture.* When judging an issue or part of one, try to see the "big picture" into which that issue fits. For example, compare the health risk from pesticides on food with other health risks.

To reduce your exposure to pesticides:

1. *Eat food grown without pesticides.* "Organic" fruits and vegetables usually have been grown without pesticides. (They may not be completely free of pesticides, however.) Such foods often cost more than foods grown with pesticides. Your family can decide whether it wants to pay this extra amount. If your market does not sell organic food, ask the manager to order it. You might also grow some of your own vegetables.

2. *Avoid "perfect" fruits and vegetables.* Some pesticides are used just to prevent slight damage to the skins of fruits and vegetables. Thus, food that looks perfect is more likely to have pesticide residues. Learn to tell harmless scars from spots that mean food is starting to spoil.

3. *Avoid fruits and vegetables that are out of season.* If you buy produce out of season—say, berries or peaches in the winter—the items probably came from another country. Imported food is safe to eat. Still, it often has more pesticides than foods grown in the United States. It is also likely to be very expensive.

4. *Wash fruits and vegetables before eating.* Use a brush and cold running water but no soap. Throw away outer leaves of vegetables such as lettuce. Peel fruits when you can.

5. *Use less pesticide in your home.* First, try to keep pests out. Put food and trash (especially food waste) in sealed containers. Empty and clean trash containers often. Seal cracks that pests can hide in or enter through. Put up screens to keep flying insects out. If you do have pests, try to control them without pesticides. Comb dogs or cats with a flea comb to get rid of fleas. Use sticky flypaper or flyswatters to kill flying insects. If you use pesticides, use relatively harmless ones like boric

acid. Use enclosed baits rather than sprays. If a pest control operator treats your home, ask if a treatment without pesticides can be used. If the operator uses a pesticide, ask what health measures you should follow after the treatment, such as opening windows.

6. *Use less pesticide in your lawn and garden.* Cover unplanted parts of your yard with pebbles or bark chips to slow weed growth. If weeds do come up, pull them instead of using herbicide. Use barriers to keep pests away from plants. Put up nest boxes or bird feeders to attract insect-eating birds. Grow plants that insect enemies of pests like. If you use pesticides, use ones like oils, Bt sprays, or neem. They are less likely to harm nonpests than stronger chemicals.

7. *If you use pesticides, do so with care.* Follow all instructions on the label. Avoid using pesticides near food. Never leave pesticide containers where children can reach them. Store and discard containers in accordance with the instructions on the label.

Glossary

Acceptable Daily Intake (ADI): The total amount of a chemical that the EPA thinks is safe for a person to consume each day in food; usually 1/100 of the No Observed Effect Level (NOEL), adjusted for body weight.

active ingredient: The part of a pesticide mixture that kills pests.

Alar: A growth-regulating chemical used on apples and some other fruit to control ripening; its chemical name is daminozide.

biological control: A form of pest control that uses one or more living things to control another.

biopesticide: A pesticide made from living things or chemicals that come from living things.

Bordeaux (bohr DOH) mixture: A mixture of copper sulfate and lime, used as a fungicide.

brown planthopper: A pest insect that attacks rice plants in Asia; it became a major pest only after pesticides wiped out its enemies.

Bt: *Bacillus thuringiensis;* a bacterium that kills insects and is used in biological control.

calcium: A mineral that makes bones and eggshells hard.

carbamates: A group of nerve-poison insecticides that includes carbofuran.

carcinogen: Something that can cause cancer.

crop rotation: Planting different crops in the same field in different years.

cultural control: A form of pest control that involves the way crops are grown or cultivated.

DDT: An organochlorine that was the first modern pesticide; short for dichlorodiphenyltrichloroethane.

Delaney Clause: A 1958 amendment to the Pure Food and Drug Act that prohibits the addition to food of a detectable amount of a carcinogen.

dose: The amount of a chemical received by a person or animal at one time.

economic damage threshold: The level of pest damage at which active pest control should be started in an IPM program; less than the economic injury level.

economic injury level: The level of pest damage at which the value of lost crops or other goods starts to be greater than the cost of controlling the pests; IPM programs try to keep losses below this level.

Environmental Protection Agency (EPA): A U.S. federal government agency set up in 1970 to regulate pesticides and other matters concerning the environment.

FIFRA: The Federal Insecticide, Fungicide, and Rodenticide Act, passed in 1947; the chief federal law that regulates pesticides.

fire ant: A pest insect in the South that can give a painful bite and sometimes damage farm machines; the USDA sprayed millions of acres with insecticides in an attempt to wipe out the fire ant in the late 1950s.

formulation: The mixture of active and inert ingredients in a commercial pesticide; also, the process of making up a mixture of active and inert ingredients that is ready to be used as a pesticide.

fungicide: A pesticide that kills fungi.

fungus (plural *fungi*): A plantlike living thing; some kinds cause plant diseases.

gene: A unit of inherited information; each body cell contains thousands of genes.

genetic: Inherited through information in the cells of living things.

genetic engineering: The scientific process of transferring genes directly from one kind of living thing to another.

gypsy moth: A serious pest, brought from Europe to the United States in 1869; it eats leaves of oaks and other shade trees.

herbicide: A pesticide that kills plants, usually weeds.

inert ingredient: Part of a commercial pesticide that does not kill pests but helps the active ingredient dissolve, spread, or stick.

Integrated Pest Management (IPM): The pest control philosophy that centers on using a variety of control techniques in the same program; pesticides are included but are used only when pest populations reach high levels.

larvae (singular *larva*): The wormlike young of many insects; for example, caterpillars are butterfly or moth larvae.

lice (singular *louse*): Tiny pests that live on the bodies of humans or animals, suck blood, and can carry diseases such as typhus.

locust: A kind of grasshopper that sometimes flies in great swarms and devours large quantities of food crops in a short time.

maximum tolerated dose: The largest amount of a chemical that animals can take in at one time and still live out their normal life span.

molting: Shedding the skin; insects must do this several times in their lives.

monoculture: The farming practice of filling large areas with the same crop year after year.

mutation: A change in a gene.

neem: A kind of tree found in Africa, India, and Asia that contains natural pesticides.

negligible risk: An EPA standard defined as the risk of up to one more cancer case per million people than would occur anyway from other causes; sometimes applied in determining how much of a carcinogen is to be allowed in food.

No Observed Effect Level (NOEL): The largest dose of a chemical (per unit of body weight) that seems to cause no damage to test animals.

no-till farming: The practice of using herbicides rather than plowing or tilling to remove weeds before crops come up.

organic food: Usually, food that has been grown without using pesticides; some organic farmers, however, use "natural" pesticides.

organochlorines: Pesticides containing the element chlorine; DDT, aldrin, and dieldrin are examples.

organophosphates: Pesticides containing the element phosphorus; parathion and malathion are examples.

parasite: A living thing that exists in or on another living thing, which it uses for food while the host is still alive.

Paris green: A compound of arsenic and copper, first used as a pesticide in Europe in the mid-nineteenth century.

pest: A plant or animal that competes with humans for food or other resources.

pesticide: Something that kills pests; usually a chemical.

pesticide treadmill: The vicious circle in which a pesticide is used, pests become resistant to it, more pesticide is then used, resistance increases, and so on.

pheromone: A chemical naturally produced by animals, especially insects, to send messages, such as cues for mating, over distance.

pyrethroids: Artificial pesticides related to a natural pesticide (pyrethrum) made by a kind of chrysanthemum.

registration: In the case of pesticides, approval by the EPA; required before a pesticide may be sold in the United States.

residue: The amount of a pesticide or other chemical remaining on food at the time the food is ready to be eaten.

scale insect: A small insect that is a pest on citrus and some other kinds of trees.

spore: A body, produced by certain bacteria and some other living things, that encloses genetic material in a protective coat.

tolerance: The amount of a possibly dangerous chemical allowed in food.

2,4-D: An herbicide that makes weeds grow abnormally and die.

USDA: U.S. Department of Agriculture; the federal agency that controls matters related to farming.

weevil: A small beetle with a long snout; some kinds are pests, while others are used to control pests.

Organizations to Contact

The following organizations have information about pesticides and pesticide use. Many of them have strong opinions about whether pesticides are safe or useful. The addresses and phone numbers are provided to help you obtain more information directly from the organizations.

Bio-Integral Resource Center (BIRC)
Box 7414
Berkeley, CA 94707
(510) 524-2567

This group provides information on applying least toxic methods of pest control, particularly in the form of Integrated Pest Management (IPM) programs. It offers a variety of low-cost publications describing what IPM is and how it may be used in different situations.

Chemical Specialties Manufacturers Association, Inc.
1001 Connecticut Ave. NW
Washington, DC 20036
(202) 872-8110

This group is made up of companies that manufacture pesticides for home and garden use.

National Agricultural Chemicals Association (NACA)
1155 Fifteenth St. NW
Washington, DC 20005
(202) 296-1585

This group promotes farm use of pesticides, artificial fertilizers, and other chemicals. It offers free publications explaining the usefulness of pesticides in farming and how a new pesticide is developed.

National Coalition Against the Misuse of Pesticides (NCAMP)
701 E St. SE, Suite 200
Washington, DC 20003
(202) 543-5450

This organization is a coalition of health, environmental, farm, consumer, and other groups and individuals who seek to focus public attention on the problems of pesticide poisoning. It works to promote pest control strategies that use few or no pesticides. It will send a variety of free publications, including its newsletter, *Pesticides and You.*

National Pest Control Association, Inc. (NPCA)
8100 Oak St.
Dunn Loring, VA 22027
(703) 573-8330

This group is made up of professional pest control operators, people who are licensed to apply dangerous pesticides. Most work in homes or large buildings in cities. NPCA will send a variety of free publications discussing the importance of pesticides and pest control in preserving health, describing ways to use pesticides safely in the home, and explaining why the group feels environmentalists are wrong to doubt the safety of pesticides.

Northwest Coalition for Alternatives to Pesticides
Box 1393
Eugene, OR 97440
(503) 344-5044

This group works to reduce pesticide use and educate people about pest control methods that do not use pesticides. It supports IPM programs and focuses on use of IPM in schools. It offers publications about IPM and alternative pest control methods for schools and homes.

Pesticide Action Network (PAN)
North American Regional Center
116 New Montgomery, #810
San Francisco, CA 94105
(415) 541-9140

PAN is an international coalition of citizens' groups in more than sixty countries. It urges adoption of methods of pest control and pesticide use that do not harm the environment or health. Its quarterly newsletter, *The Global Pesticide Campaigner*, is available by subscription. PAN will send back issues and some other publications free.

Rachel Carson Council, Inc.
8940 Jones Mill Rd.
Chevy Chase, MD 20815
(301) 652-1877

Founded by one of Rachel Carson's personal friends, this group tries to carry on the late naturalist's work by promoting pesticide safety and warning people about the dangers of many pesticides. It will send a variety of free publications about possible dangers of pesticides to wildlife and human health.

Suggestions for Further Reading

Doc Abraham and Katy Abraham, "Guide to Organic Pesticides," *Mother Earth News*, February/March 1994.

Frances Bequette, "Can the World Feed Itself Without Chemicals?" *UNESCO Courier*, April 1993.

Rachel Carson, *Silent Spring*. Boston: Houghton Mifflin, 1962.

Daniel Jack Chasan, "How Ya Gonna Keep Bugs Down (on the Farm)?" *Smithsonian*, January 1979.

Anne Witte Garland, *For Our Kids' Sake*. San Francisco: Sierra Club Books, 1989.

"Getting the Bugs Out: How to Control Household Pests," *Consumer Reports*, July 1993.

Frank Graham Jr., *The Dragon Hunters*. New York: Dutton, 1984.

————, *Since Silent Spring*. Boston: Houghton Mifflin, 1970.

Dwight Holing, "Looking for Mr. Goodbug," *Sierra*, January/February 1990.

"How to Read Pesticide Labels," *Consumers' Research*, July 1992.

William Jordan, "Phenomena, Comment and Notes," *Smithsonian*, March 1991.

"The Joy Ride Is Over," *U.S. News & World Report*, September 14, 1992.

Jeanne McDermott, "Some Heartland Farmers Just Say No to Chemicals," *Smithsonian*, April 1990.

Joanna Poncavage, "Sold on Organic," *Organic Gardening*, June 1989.

David Warner, "The Food Industry Takes the Offensive," *Nation's Business*, July 1991.

Pamela Weintraub, "The Coming of the High-Tech Harvest," *Audubon*, July/August 1992.

Jamie L. Whitten, *That We May Live*. New York: Van Nostrand, 1966.

Works Consulted

"Alar: Not Gone, Not Forgotten," *Consumer Reports,* May 1989.

Christopher J. Bosso, *Pesticides and Politics: The Life Cycle of a Public Issue.* Pittsburgh: University of Pittsburgh Press, 1987.

Shirley A. Briggs and the staff of Rachel Carson Council, *Basic Guide to Pesticides: Their Characteristics and Hazards.* Washington, DC: Taylor & Francis, 1992.

Paul Debach and David Rosen, *Biological Control by Natural Enemies.* Cambridge: Cambridge University Press, 1991.

"Does Everything Cause Cancer?" *Consumers' Research,* May 1989.

W. W. Fletcher, *The Pest War.* New York: Wiley, 1974.

M. L. Flint and R. van den Bosch, *Introduction to Integrated Pest Management.* New York: Plenum, 1981.

"Forbidden Fruit?" *Harvard Health Letter,* January 1994.

Judith E. Foulke, "Pesticide Residues in Your Children's Food," *Consumers' Research,* August 1993.

Leonard Gianessi, "Why Chemical-Free Farming Won't Work," *Consumers' Research,* December 1993.

Michael Hansen, *Escape from the Pesticide Treadmill: Alternatives to Pesticides in Developing Countries.* New York: International Organization of Consumers Unions, 1987.

Bart Lambert and Marnix Peferoen, "Insecticidal Promise of *Bacillus thuringiensis,*" *BioScience,* February 1992.

Reed McManus, "Trusting to Luck," *Sierra,* January/February 1994.

Robert L. Metcalf and William H. Luckmann, eds., *Introduction to Insect Pest Management,* 2nd ed. New York: Wiley, 1982.

George Ordish, *The Constant Pest.* New York: Scribner's, 1976.

David Pimentel et al., "Benefits and Risks of Genetic Engineering in Agriculture," *BioScience,* October 1989.

————, "Environmental and Economic Costs of Pesticide Use," *BioScience,* November 1992.

John P. Reganold et al., "Sustainable Agriculture," *Scientific American,* June 1990.

Leslie Roberts, "Alar: The Numbers Game," *Science,* March 17, 1989.

Joseph V. Rodricks, *Calculated Risks.* Cambridge: Cambridge University Press, 1992.

Leslie Spencer, "Ban All Plants—They Pollute," *Forbes,* October 25, 1993.

Peter D. Stiling, *An Introduction to Insect Pests and Their Control.* New York: Macmillan, 1985.

Richard Stone, "A Biopesticidal Tree Begins to Bloom," *Science,* February 28, 1992.

————, "Researchers Score Victory over Pesticides—and Pests—in Asia," *Science,* May 29, 1992.

U.S. General Accounting Office, "Pesticides: 30 Years Since *Silent Spring,* Many Long-Standing Concerns Remain." Report, July 23, 1992.

Diana West, "Taking Aim at a Deadly Chemical," *National Wildlife,* June/July 1992.

James Whorton, *Before Silent Spring.* Princeton, NJ: Princeton University Press, 1974.

David Zilberman et al., "The Economics of Pesticide Use and Regulation," *Science,* January 2, 1991.

Index

About the Author

Lisa Yount earned a bachelor's degree with honors in English and Creative Writing from Stanford University. She has a lifelong interest in nature and biology and is a nature guide at the Terwilliger Nature Education Center in Corte Madera. She has been a professional writer and editor for more than twenty-five years, producing mostly educational materials, magazine articles, and books for young people. This is her twelfth book. She lives in El Cerrito, California, with her husband.

Picture Credits

DREAMING OF DISNEY

John Lasseter started dreaming about working for Disney his first year in high school. After reading a book called *The Art of Animation* he found in the school library, he realized that people could have jobs as animation artists. Not long after that, he went to see a Disney movie, *The Sword in the Stone*, at a local theater. When his mom picked him up afterward, he told her that he wanted to work for Disney. That dream led Lasseter, who was voted "best artist" by his classmates, to attend the California Institute of Arts after graduation. He was offered a job at Disney while he was still in school and worked there from 1979 until 1983, when he was fired. By the time Lasseter returned to Disney in 2006, he had made a name for himself as one of the most gifted, creative computer animation artists in the industry.

GLOSSARY

acquisition the purchase of one company by another

animator a person who prepares the artwork for animated, or not live-action, films

board of directors a group of people in charge of making decisions for a publicly owned company

competition organizations that try to get the business or attention of the same group of customers

credits a list acknowledging the contributors to a movie or television program that is scrolled down the screen at the end of the program

debt money that is owed to a bank or other lender

desktop publishing the production of printed material from a printer linked to a desktop computer that uses software on the computer to create documents

engineers people who design, build, and maintain systems for specific uses

executives decision-making leaders of a company, such as the president or chief executive officer (CEO)

initial public offering a company's first opportunity for the public to purchase shares of ownership

investment banks financial institutions that purchase shares of companies or other organizations in exchange for ownership in that company or organization

patents government-granted rights that allow an individual or company to make, use, or sell specific products or technology

photorealistic a detailed representation of something that appears to be almost photographic

piracy the unauthorized use or reproduction of someone else's work

profit the amount of money that a business keeps after subtracting expenses from income

rendering the use of color and shading to make the outline of an object appear solid and three-dimensional

revenue the money earned by a company; another word for income

screenwriters people who write the screenplays, or stories, for television shows and movies

script the written text of a play, movie, or other broadcast that includes the lines spoken by all the characters

share one of the equal parts a company may be divided into; shareholders each hold a certain number of shares, or a percentage, of the company

shareholder people or corporations who own shares of stock (portions of ownership in a corporation)

short a movie lasting 30 minutes or less; from the early 1900s to the 1950s, shorts were often shown before a full-length movie

software written programs or rules that control a computer's operations

stock shared ownership in a company by many people who buy shares, or portions, of stock, hoping the company will make a profit and the stock value will increase

venture capital funds made available to small businesses that are starting out but show great potential for growth

SELECTED BIBLIOGRAPHY

Capodagli, Bill, and Lynn Jackson. *Innovate the Pixar Way: Business Lessons from the World's Most Creative Corporate Playground.* New York: McGraw-Hill, 2009.

IMDb.com. "The List of Pixar Movies and Short Movies." http://www.imdb.com/list/jEPQZX6lxuU/.

Paik, Karen. *To Infinity and Beyond!: The Story of Pixar Animation Studios.* San Francisco: Chronicle Books, 2007.

Pixar. "Our Story." http://www.pixar.com/about/Our-Story.

Price, David A. *The Pixar Touch.* New York: Knopf, 2008.

Ratzenberger, John. "TIME 100: John Lasseter." *TIME,* April 21, 2011.

Note: Every effort has been made to ensure that any websites listed above were active at the time of publication. However, because of the nature of the Internet, it is impossible to guarantee that these sites will remain active indefinitely or that their contents will not be altered.

INDEX